The Seven Elemental Forces of Huna

The Seven Elemental Forces of Huna

*Practices for Tapping into
the Energies of Nature
from the Hawaiian Tradition*

Susanne Weikl

EARTHDANCER

AN INNER TRADITIONS IMPRINT

First edition 2019
Susanne Weikl
The Seven Elemental Forces of Huna:
Practices for Tapping into the Energies of Nature

This English edition © Earthdancer GmbH 2019
English translation © 2018 JMS books LLP
Editing by JMS books LLP (www.jmseditorial.com)
Originally published as: *Energiequelle Natur: Mit den Naturkräften leicht durch den Alltag*
World © Neue Erde GmbH, Saarbruecken, Germany 2018

Cover design: DesignIsIdentity.com
Cover photography: Willyam Bradberry/shutterstock.com
Typesetting and layout: DesignIsIdentity.com
Typeset in Whitman and Myriad
Printed and bound in China by Midas Printing Ltd.

ISBN 978-1-62055-885-0 (print)
ISBN 978-1-62055-886-7 (e-book)

Published by Earthdancer, an imprint of Inner Traditions
www.earthdancerbooks.com, www.innertraditions.com

MIX
Paper from
responsible sources
FSC® C137129
FSC
www.fsc.org

He 'olina leo ka ke Aloha

Joy is in the voice of love

CONTENTS

AN EASIER LIFE

Do you dream of finding it easier to cope with daily life?

Would you like to:
- have enough energy left to enjoy your evenings, instead of crashing out on the couch,
- start your vacations in a relaxed frame of mind, instead of feeling sick and stressed,
- look forward to weekends with enthusiasm, instead of dragging yourself home on a Friday,
- take life easier, finding useful solutions to problems instead of trudging around in circles with the weight of the world on your shoulders,
- come across as confident and relaxed, instead of being timid and reserved,
- have a great source of strength at your side at all times, instead of having to manage your energy reserves carefully?

This dream can come true, and the solution is closer than you think. My advice is to make use of the energy sources Nature has to offer. Open your eyes, look around you, and recognize the forces that are there every day, waiting to help you. In this book, I will show you how you can tap into the elemental forces of Nature sustainably, effortlessly, and creatively in your day-to-day life.

Make your day easier, create reserves of energy, and learn to work with the elemental forces of Nature on an equal footing.

Simply being aware that the energies of Nature are within us and all around us is not enough: to put our ideas into practice in the most effective and economical way we must use them directly and with awareness. I love looking at gardens, climbing mountains, and sitting beside the sea, of course, as Nature is all around me and I live within it. But really making use of the energies of Nature is another matter entirely; it involves shaping our lives powerfully and adroitly.

I'm a child of Nature. Even as a little girl, I loved to be outside, helping my grandmother in the garden, having fun with the dogs, collecting worms for the hens, and dreaming of playing with the pixies. That was a long time ago, but now I know about the energies of Nature and how I can tap into them in my life. It was Huna that helped me to achieve this, a way of life originating in ancient Hawaii that allowed me to study the energies of Nature intensively, and to get to know myself better in the process. I live and teach Huna in my daily life, constantly discovering new and more effective ways to integrate the elemental forces of Nature into my lifestyle. This has strengthened the bond between us, and my appreciation of the power of Nature's elemental forces and the way they govern life increases with every day. I would love to share my experiences with you and pass on my passion for shaping life using the power of the seven elemental forces of Nature.

Whatever I am doing, whether it is cleaning a burnt pan, sitting in a meeting, or trimming the hedge, the energies of Nature help me to do it as effectively and dynamically as I possibly can. I am using the best source of energy there is: the elemental forces of Nature. They boost my energy again and again. I draw on my own elemental power and work my way through the events of the day smoothly and with a spring in my step.

Whether you are a Nature lover or a couch potato, the key to your elemental nature lies within you. Forge a strong partnership with the forces that Nature possesses and you will always have a source of energy to draw on.

We humans are born to live out our full potential and to express our strength, full of dynamism and without restrictions, and in expressing such strength we can be wild, impetuous, and strong-willed, or gentle, gracious, and contemplative. This unlimited power, in all its infinite variety, is ours for the taking.

Allow yourself this partnership with the elements and explore the possibilities and new experiences that await you. Familiarize yourself with every aspect of the seven elemental forces, and you will no longer be fighting alone; your strength will be reinforced with the energy of mighty beech trees, graceful wildcats, spirited raindrops, inquisitive sunbeams, fresh sea breezes, majestic peaks, or fleet-footed angels. You will have access to resources offering wonderful opportunities, and discover what it means to be at the height of your powers. Your life will become richer in a way that will help you every single day, and best of all, you will find that you are daring to do more, and it has suddenly become easier to transform your small ideas and big plans into reality.

Very best wishes
Susanne Weikl

THE SOURCE OF ALL LIFE

Nature is the source of all life, a concept expressed most beautifully in the Hawaiian approach to life: they describe themselves as *Keiki o ka'aina*, "Children of the Land." Nature is a part of us, and we have its power within us. People and Nature are like brothers and sisters, and our mutual support is a given; our true strength has its roots in this connection based on our origins.

Feel the power of this Hawaiian legend and open yourself up to its magic. The tale of how this deep love affair between humans and Nature came about is very moving. Nothing has changed to this day. The forces of Nature are ours to use: we were born to have this source of power at our side.

An unimaginably long time ago, Wakea, the Sky Father, and Haumea, the Earth Mother, had a child together. This child was in a great hurry and was born too early, in a non-human form. Its body was in the shape of a tuber, symbolizing the hour of the birth of Nature. The Sky Father named the child Haloa, meaning "Long Breath" or "the Roots of Life." He buried the body on the eastern side of his home, where the sun came up.

The second child born to the couple was a healthy boy who would become the ancestor of the Hawaiian people. He, too, was named Haloa, in honor of his elder brother, so they would be bound together for all eternity. Nature, the older brother, would always help and nourish Humanity, while the younger brother was a reminder to people that they are a part of Nature and of Haloa, the first human.

Tapping into the energies of Nature in our daily lives is a way of returning to our roots. For me, it is the most beautiful, the most powerful, and the most environmentally friendly way of living there is, and it might soon be for you, too. Filled with joy, curiosity, and anticipation, let's bring new vitality and dynamism into your life and make room for a powerful way of living.

THE SEVEN ELEMENTAL FORCES OF NATURE

Would you like to discover your essential nature, experience how powerful you really are, and find out how courageously you can act? Then let the energies of Nature become part of your life. In Nature, we find riches in all their infinite variety: in health, healing power, dynamism, energy, joyfulness, and essential power. What could be more important than using Nature as a source of power to bring fulfillment, incentive, inspiration, growth, healing, and ease into our lives? Instead of being restrained, or having to carefully manage your reserves of energy, you can now draw on Nature's infinite source of energy.

The relationship between humans and Nature has always been an intimate love affair. Each force of Nature is a part of us and we are a part of these elements. These forces are not hidden, tamed, subdued, or dormant, even if it might seem that way from time to time. They are dynamic, powerful and primordial, self-sufficient (in a positive way), and energetic. The elements are a part of our heritage, they are at work in our DNA. They help us to manifest our ideas, to get the most out of life, and feel truly alive.

Let's start with an introduction to the way Huna sees the seven elemental forces of Nature. This will show you all the elements and how they are expressed. Huna teaches us about the power of the seven elements, but the way we choose to approach and apply this power, and the meaning we see in it, is entirely up to us. The way these qualities are allocated to each individual element is a direct result of this freedom, and a distillation of many years of my practical experience for myself and on behalf of others.

In addition to the seven elemental forces, Huna recognizes seven qualities of power. The guide that follows will show you how you can weave these aspects together. Each element is associated with a Hawaiian goddess as an expression of the truth that everything arises from a divine source. When we sit in our bathtubs, for example, we are surrounded by the goddess of water; the crackling of a fire is a melody sung by the fire-goddess Pele; and the bird at our window represents the goddess of the animals. We are surrounded by divine energy, so it is entirely natural to see ourselves as human beings of great worth. We are constantly bathed in this energy and it lends us incredible strength.

Don't be surprised that I have also listed modern manifestations of these elements among the forms in which they can present themselves: the more creative we are, the more opportunities we have to make these forces accessible at any time.

The seven energies of Nature in Huna

Element	Quality	Manifestation	Goddess
Wind	Consciousness, perception, realization	Breath, gust, breeze, storm, hurricane, fan, blow-dryer, airconditioning unit	Hi'iaka
Fire	Freedom, space, release of energy, transformation	Sun, laser, flames, hot coals, explosion, volcano, lava, lightning, stars, real fire, cooking pan, heating	Pele
Water	Focus, decisiveness, ambition	Rain, snow, ice, sea, river, waterfall, ocean, fog, steam, perspiration, domestic drinking water, well	Hina
Plants	Presence, being in the moment, timeliness, updating	Trees, flowers, herbs, bushes, moss, algae, dried flowers, logs, furniture, doors, books, pictures	Laka
Rocks	Love, praise, self-esteem, pleasure	Mountains, hills, crystals, shellfish, metals, minerals, houses, walls, towers, devices, crockery	Haumea
Animals	Creative power, autonomy, self-confidence	Mammals, reptiles, birds, fish, amphibians, mollusks, pictures, sculptures, clothing, shoes	Kapo
People	Harmony, flexibility, success	Gods, masters, teachers, ancestors, angels, light-beings, fellow humans, characters in books, magazines, films	Uli

So, let's break the ice and get to know the elements. After all, the first thing you do at a party is introduce yourself and say hello. And I am quite deliberately introducing the elements using their Hawaiian names; in the Hawaiian language a word can have many meanings, which, taken together, present a very accurate and comprehensive description of an element. A profound wisdom that I want to share with you lies hidden within.

Wind

As Shakespeare says, "Blow, blow, thou winter wind, thou art not so unkind." The wind is invisible and light as air, and yet we feel its presence. The wind is called *makani* in the Hawaiian language. This word expresses how the wind always has a destination, how it makes its presence felt with sounds, and how it can howl loudly in triumph; it can fit through the eye of a needle, has many faces, yet is always fresh, brisk, and ever-present in the ways it supports us. This is just to give you an idea of the primeval forces that the wind has in store for you. The wind is capricious, changing rapidly, and drives the other elements; the wind brings the air we breathe, as well as inspiration and communication with ourselves and with others. It carries our words out into the world and ensures we are heard. Wind appears to have no substance, it gets everywhere, it is flexible and can read our thoughts. This brings us the gift of greater awareness, sharpens our self-perception, and helps us to achieve insights.

Greeting

- Focus on the wind, or alternatively on your own breath, hearing and feeling it.
- Sense its purposefulness, its capacity for change, its expressiveness, and its presence.
- Explore how the wind interacts with the other elements and how it deals with resistance.
- Intone a syllable, and then intone the same syllable using the power of the wind to help you. Feel the difference when the wind accompanies this self-expression. Now try how it feels to speak loudly and clearly, with and without the wind.

Fire

Our hearts are on fire when we are passionate about something, and this capacity for excitement and interest is typical of the element of fire. The sun appears in the sky day after day, bringing light into our lives, and in Hawaii, fire is known as *ahi*. Fire is scorching and untamed, it burns, glows, and sizzles; it can crackle quietly or spit sparks, hiss and fizz, destroy or unite in the heat of passion. Fire represents every kind of freedom, endurance, intensity, transformation, illumination, wakefulness, and warmth. Fire is unlimited and insatiable in its vitality, it is destruction and renewal: the pure transformation and passion that brings us freedom. When we throw something into the fire, we free it from its form and issue an invitation to take on a new and better form. It is an element that couldn't have been more perfectly created for changing constraining rules.

Greeting

- Focus your attention entirely on the sun or another source of fire. In what form do you sense the power of fire?
- Forge a link between yourself and the freedom, passion, intensity, and brilliance of the fire.
- Explore the power of the fire that is within you; how brightly does it shine?
- Your stomach is the nexus of your digestion, of transformation within you. Boost the fire of your digestion with the power of the sun, of a volcano, or with another source of fire.

Water

No one wants to lead their life feeling like a "fish out of water." Water can take any form, it shapes the world around it, and has a close connection with our emotions. In the Hawaiian language the word for water is *wai*, while *waiwai* means wealth and recognition in every conceivable sense of the word. Water brings life and sustains the living, it is the essence of lifeblood, living force, semen, and can take on any color. It gives, it glides, it flows, it enriches and positions itself; water is our element—we are two-thirds water. We express our joy and suffering with tears; water surrounds us in the womb and supports us as it flows through our lives. It can deal with any obstructions, changing and reshaping obstacles gently and with perseverance, and is constantly in motion, even when dammed up. Water never changes its course; it is the source of concentration and orientation. It helps us to demonstrate decisiveness and to get down to work with a clear goal in mind.

Greeting

- Make physical contact with water: place your hands or feet in a bowl of water and sense your link with this life-giving liquid.
- Explore the element of water contained within you: are you flowing freely?
- Imagine you are a wide river. Feel your flow and sense how you encounter other elements.
- Heal yourself with water. Hold a glass of water in your hand and fill it with beautiful thoughts. Drink the water and focus on allowing these thoughts to flow into every single cell of your body.

Plants

We have strong roots, we "pull chestnuts out of the fire" and we "touch wood," all of which express our strong connection with plants. Plants cleanse our air, delight our senses, and are our principal source of nourishment. The Hawaiian word *la'au* describes how plants heal and bring blessings; how they come into bloom and seek the sun, and how they contain sun and warmth within themselves; how they show us the time of day and the passing of time; how they are in the present moment and experience sensations. Plants are inherent and show their presence in all kinds of forms and colors; a tiny violet burgeons with exactly the same degree of self-confidence as a mighty tree. They are rooted in the ground and grow upward toward the sky; they want to flourish, bloom, reproduce, and fill space. Plants are the best teachers for being in the here and now, for consciously experiencing every moment. They remind us to continually "update" our ideas of ourselves, to live the newest version of ourselves and not get bogged down in past roles and experiences.

Greeting

- Look at the plants around you: what species and varieties do you have in your home? Which plant came into your head first? What presence does it radiate?

- There is more plant-based inspiration behind being human than we might imagine: we grow, we bloom, our work bears fruit, and we put down roots. Explore the plant-like elements within you: how much room do you have to grow and bloom?

- Examine your current situation: are any shadows of the past casting a pall over your aura right now?

- Find a plant that for you radiates a presence, then think of a situation in which you feel small. Place the plant behind you and see how your perception of the situation changes.

Rocks

"Sticks and stones may break our bones," but a person can be "our rock." Rocks are unmistakable; we walk across them and they provide a foothold. *Pohaku* describes how rocks are adept at arranging and folding themselves into strata, can stand erect and anchor themselves firmly in life, and yet can explode and break; their cracks and crevices form their character. They breathe and store a memory of the history of the world. Rocks are the bones of the Earth, and we are connected to the Earth through our bones. They exist peacefully on their own terms, with clear boundaries and hidden treasures. Rocks are ever-present in our lives, a stable and constant reminder that the force in the universe that unites everything is love. They know their own value, they are without pretence and are content.

Greeting

- Stand with both feet planted firmly on the ground and feel the bones of the Earth. After a minute or two, focus your attention on the bones of your own body: how do you perceive them now?

- Rocks are a symbol of love as a uniting force. The next time you go for a walk, think about how you could be absorbing this love with every step you take.

- Hold a crystal in your hand and feel its stability, letting it flow into your body until you feel safe and grounded.

- Rocks tell stories. Find a pebble and look at its shape, texture, and surface: what does it make you think about?

Animals

We "take the bull by the horns" and we shirk from mentioning "the elephant in the room"; sheep's wool and goose down keep us warm; bees fertilize flowers; cats and dogs comfort us when we feel down; pigs and goats provide us with food.

Holoholona teaches us that animals are able to make swift decisions, display great resolve, walk, run, and hunt, but also to relax, doze, and eventually take their rest. The best way I can think of to describe animals is as creatures taking full pleasure in the world. They are highly skilled at adapting and surviving, and can teach us to be flexible and to trust our instincts when we act; they are excellent navigators, supporting their communities in all kinds of ways, and they are proud but not vain. Animals radiate self-confidence and invite us to bring our best sides to the fore. They reinforce our autonomy (independence in the positive sense) and remind us of how powerful we are.

Greeting

- Choose an animal whose beauty you admire. How does it move through the world?
- Choose an animal that you are scared of or find repulsive. What qualities does this animal have?
- How powerful do you perceive yourself to be? What influence do you have on your life?
- Reinforce your power in a situation in which you feel unsure. What animal could help you here? Feel its power at your back.

People

We describe our fellow human beings as angels when they provide us with selfless support; we idolize another person, or hope for divine inspiration. Gods, angels, masters, teachers, light-beings, ancestors, and our fellow humans are all at our side, helping us to become more mature and more perfect. *Uli*, the goddess of the human element, is the divinity of the magical arts and of healing; she has enormous influence and power to shape events. She has the power to kill and the power to bring things back to life. Her home is the land beyond the horizon, and she reminds us that we carry the divine spark within us and can decide whether to choose the path of harmony or of strife. We are all angels, masters, teachers, and wise human beings, yet at the same time also apprentices, pupils, trainees, and novices aspiring one day to be clever and wise. Deep inside each human being is the potential to use creative magic to shape their life in the best possible way. As magicians and healers, we are flexible and can make use of balance and harmony, so that at the end of our lives we are able to say, "In my own way, I tried to bring greater harmony to everything that I did in my life."

Greeting

- Have you ever thought of yourself as a goddess of magic or healing? How does it feel to have such powers?
- What kind of magic do you admire, and what can you "pull out of a hat" with ease?
- Think of someone whom you idolize, admire, or revere. What is the secret of their success?
- If you were an angel, how would you look, and what would be your special ability?

You have greeted all the elements, become acquainted with them, and got to know them better. Each element brings an individual power and wisdom with it; you will be able to sense which you should choose, depending on the situation.

BRINGING YOUR POWER CIRCLE TO LIFE

In the course of my work with the energies of Nature, I have created a power circle for myself that I can use for any purpose, and many people have followed my example. I like to activate this power circle as soon as I wake up, so that I begin my day at the height of my powers. Now that you have become familiar with the seven elements, the time has come to strengthen and stabilize the contact you have made. Take time out for this special moment as you will be bringing your own power circle to life. The power circle is an expression of your deepest desire to live from this moment on in the closest possible contact with the elements.

The ritual that follows will allow you to create a firm basis for your work with the energies of Nature. This power circle is the core of your being, your starting point, your home base. Wherever you happen to be, whatever the season, this power circle of the elements will always be with you; you can have recourse to it whenever you need it.

This ritual will be all the more beautiful and moving, with a greater intensity of feeling, if you take your time and throw yourself into it wholeheartedly. Consider each element in turn, being sensitive to which form this element would like to take in your power circle. You could follow this order: wind – fire – water – plants – rocks – animals – people. Take your time and wait until you know whether you are going to integrate the element of wind as a fresh breeze, a howling easterly, or a hot sirocco. Each of the seven elements should feature once. When you have been once round the circle, you will have created your own individual circle of the elements. My current power circle as described below may give you some ideas for arranging your own.

Exercise: Create a power circle of the elements

This is my power circle of the elements.

As you can see, all the elements are represented in a form that suits me for the time being. I can, of course, change the form in which they occur at any time.

1st station wind: stiff breeze

2nd station fire: active volcano

3rd station water: a pleasant, temperate, tropical waterfall

4th station plants: a luscious coconut palm with coconuts

5th station rocks: Mauna Kea, the majestic mountain of Hawaii

6th station animals: a cheerful, cheeky dolphin

7th station people: an airy, breezy light-being

Taking these as your inspiration, close your eyes and start to give shape to your power circle. When your circle is finished, place yourself in the center with the aim of feeling safe and at peace, and perceive its special power. You can use this circle for all the exercises in this book and in every aspect of your life.

Presenting your power circle

Each of us has different talents and our own way of giving the elements a clear place in our lives. Some people might visualize vivid images; others might be creative and artistically gifted; others again might prefer to have things set out clearly in front of them. There are all kinds of ways to visualize your power circle for yourself:

1. Vizualize vivid, colorful images in your mind that you can experience with all your senses and conjure up any time.

2. Make a picture or a collage of your power circle on canvas and find a suitable place for it in your home. It's best if you can position it so that you can sit directly in front of your artwork and have an uninterrupted view of it.

3. If you'd prefer to have your power circle in your garden, make a kind of mandala with all the elements you need, leaving space in the middle for yourself.

4. Look through your photographs, or search the internet, and print out color images of your elements. Lay out these pictures in a convenient place that allows you to assemble a circle quickly when required, and then position yourself in the middle.

5. Using your own Nature photographs, make a photo-collage online and turn it into a poster that you can hang up.

6. Set up your power circle where you meditate. Find objects that symbolize the elements: a candle, a water bowl, or a stone, for example.

7. If you often go out into Nature and like to visit the same place, set up your power circle there. Perhaps take a photograph of the place so that you can use your power circle even when you're not there.

I'm sure you will have plenty more ideas of ways to make your power circle an important place in your life. All you need is to get started and the inspiration will flow.

Strengthening the bond

Forging an ever-closer relationship with the individual elements in your circle is a great experience. In time, it will be easy to make contact and you'll feel as if you're visiting old friends. Enter your circle at regular intervals and spend some time with each element to strengthen your relationship with it. This is an excellent way of recharging your batteries. Having a properly established power circle is ideal for when you don't have much time or you need support quickly. Never again will you have to spend time looking around you for strength and support, you can go straight to the center of your power and seek help.

With every tour of the circle, you will assimilate the elements and their order; life is movement, and your power circle isn't static: it's very much alive. Be flexible in swapping the forms the elements take to manifest themselves, play around with them, and don't be afraid of making spontaneous changes. Variety is the spice of life.

Practical tips

I believe that the more flexible we are, the more benefit we can draw from the energies of Nature. Whenever I feel the desire to work with the forces at play at any given time, I do just that; it brings a new dynamic to my actions. Right now, I have writer's block, so I discover the wind that is blowing in through the window; Pele, the fire

goddess, is hanging on the wall; there is a cup of water on the desk; my wooden chair is bringing me the power of plants; my computer represents the essence of stones; I am sitting on a cushion made of sheepskin, and an angel sits on a bookshelf. This union of the elements brings me new energy and my fingers are once again flying over the keyboard. My basic power circle is always the same, I am just using a different version at the moment.

Whenever I am outside, I take note of what is around me and make a power circle from what I see. So the air I breathe, the warmth of a sunbeam, the dewdrops on the grass, the orchid in the window of a house, the wall surrounding the window, the ants on the ground, and the nymph inhabiting a tree might come together to form my power circle. If I'm driving to the store and trying to think of a solution to a problem, I make a power circle from the air rushing past, the warmth of the engine, raindrops, a patch of grass, the road surface, my dog, and my guardian angel to find a good outcome.

If I need a boost during a healing therapy, I will combine the summer wind, a burning candle, a water glass, a rosebush, the floor of the room, and the patient's guardian angel to make a power circle. I don't spend too long thinking about it, I just take the first thing that comes into my head; that's how flexible we can be when we work with the energies of Nature, whether inside or out in the fresh air. Isn't that wonderful?

Exercise: Make conscious use of the elements

By now you should be making use of the qualities of the individual elements, so think of circumstances in which you could apply these. Place yourself in your power circle and call to the wind. Wrap this wind around yourself, focusing exclusively on your conscious perceptions and realizations about the issue that come to mind.

Having achieved these insights, add the element of fire to your circle and see how much freedom and passion it inspires in your thoughts and how much further it takes them. Now it's time for water, which will help you to achieve clearer and better focus, and to make a decision. Take this focus with you to your plant power; now is the time to be in the moment and to let go of the baggage of the past. In order to be constant, a focus requires love and praise; your rock element will provide this love. The animal you have chosen will ensure you have the power to apply this new focus in your life; take as much energy as you need. Finally, the human element is the crowning glory:

it provides the necessary harmony and flexibility to round off this ritual and to integrate the healing process into your life.

Real-life accounts

Petra

I am sitting in my power circle and a gentle sea breeze is caressing me. I have had a cough for a while and my whole chest area hurts. The wind is showing dark green patches on the lower part of my torso that are dissolving here and there, and then coming back; they have a sticky and slimy consistency, it reminds me of seaweed.

I call upon fire, the sun, surrounding myself with it. At first, I only see a few individual points of light, but I can gradually make out the sun more and more clearly. I then work with the element of water: I am standing in a wide river because I want to see the whole of the sun, dissolve the mist, and be able to breathe without pain again. I can feel the pain at the edges of my torso. I want to be able to speak freely. To speak freely: yes, that's exactly what I want. Images from the past rise up, helped by thoughts of my rosebushes. I hold myself back in quarrels, I don't speak my mind. I am only in the moment when I express what moves me. I go to the foot of my mountain, breathe in deeply, and connect with the love that is stored in this great rock, love of myself. I let it stream through my entire chest. What I need now is the strength of my orangutan, so that I can have faith in my own autonomy, as well as really daring to speak my mind. My guardian angel is the last stop on my journey; he whispers words into my ear that bring me an enormous sense of wellbeing. I feel good, nourished, strong, and ready to practice speaking as I choose.

Ellen

My desk is in an open-plan office and things always get pretty hectic in our department, particularly toward the end of the month. On days like that, I set up a power circle around me so I can concentrate better on work. For wind, I use my breath; the ceiling lights are fire; my vacation snapshots provide the power of water; the beech hedge in front of the building represents the power of plants; my computer stands in for the solid element of rocks; I take the power of animals from my shoes, and the Buddha on my desk rounds things off nicely. Since working with the circle, I'm not so exhausted in the evenings and I no longer suffer from tension headaches.

Instead of working with your entire power circle, you can work with just one individual element. Here are a few examples to inspire you:

- You are racking your brains and failing to come up with any ideas: the wind can help you.
- You want to change an unwritten rule: fire will give you the passion to do so.
- You don't know what decision to make: use the power of water.
- You are stuck in the past: get in touch with the present once more through a plant.
- You feel as if people are looking right through you, ignoring you: give yourself the gift of the love and appreciation of your rock.
- You daren't make changes to anything: get in touch with your animal element.
- You can't see beyond a particular solution: take advice from a divine being.

The examples opposite are some ways in which you can use the power of the elements for yourself and for your life. There are plenty more in the rest of this book.

TOOLS FOR TAKING DYNAMIC ACTION

In this book you will discover Huna, a tried and tested Hawaiian guide for powerful connection to and communication with the elemental forces of Nature. I have been inspired for many years by the versatile techniques and approaches to be found in this philosophy. If you need some encouragement to integrate the energies of Nature into your life, just remind yourself that it is easy; be bold, everything you need to do this is within you.

In this chapter, I will introduce you to a range of approaches and techniques that will lay down good foundations, help you gain easy access to the energies of Nature, and enjoy a relaxed dialogue with them. Integrating the exercises into your life will help you translate this into immediate action.

Laying good foundations

A positive attitude

It's very easy to make a connection with the elemental forces of Nature, and most people have no difficulty communicating with them. Each of us has possessed this ability since childhood. This fundamental idea has helped me to guide and mentor any number of people in seminars in Nature, and to ensure they achieve the same success.

I was recently reading a children's book with my four-year-old nephew about a little hare who left home and moved away. Wherever the hare went, however, no one was allowed to tickle his ears; only his mom could do that. My nephew has a soft toy hare, and he thought for a little while about whether he would be allowed to tickle its ears. He concentrated hard on Mr Hare and then shook his head decisively. When I asked him how he could be so certain, he said he had simply asked Mr Hare. It's just as simple and obvious for us adults too, but instead of toys, we will communicate with trees, rivers, and plants. Let's bring out the child within us and make use of our natural abilities. You might find it a little hard to start with, but with practice and support from Nature, you will soon make progress. I have chosen two exercises that will help you to reactivate your childlike qualities.

Exercise: Awaken your playful side

We play because we have a desire for new experiences. Just watch children: the urge to play is immediately obvious. There is a playful person inside each and every one of us. What games do you like to play? It might be social games, sports games, solving puzzles, bamboozling people, planning surprises, or games as simple as sitting in a café and trying to guess which passers-by will turn their heads to look at you. What does playing mean to you, and what satisfaction and joy can you find in it?

Exercise: Free your elemental nature

Society today takes a dim view of emotional outbursts, such as the stamping of feet or whoops of joy. So let's free our elemental natures from today's restrictive attitude. To do this, find a good spot outdoors, somewhere where the energies of Nature can be expressed freely. A place where you are surrounded by lush and luxuriant plants, somewhere on a windswept hill, or among animals would be ideal. Breathe in all Nature's elemental force and enjoy its wild power. Now you can be impetuous, loud, and feel deep emotions again—quite simply, Nature's primal force in all its forms.

Thinking of Nature as family

Nature is not a place we visit; it's our home, our family, where we live. We humans are fire, water, wind, earth, plants, animals, and light-beings. Everything in Nature has the power to shape its own life; it has a soul, it is alive, it is conscious and can be communicated with, so it follows that it's possible to establish a connection with every element. When we tap into the energies of Nature, we develop a deeper understanding of who we are and come to know ourselves in a new way.

Ritual: Get to know your family

This ritual will help you discover who you are, what you are made of, and where you come from. If you have the opportunity, conduct the ritual outdoors, for example, while out walking. As you stroll along, take in all the elements with each of your senses and be aware that all the elements are within you; so a beech tree, a daisy, a raindrop, a pebble, a bird, a seed, a flash of light, and the west wind are all part of you and have a connection with you. Whether you take a walk in reality or just in your mind, it is a path to power and to creating power. Your energy levels will rise and you will find it easier to dream. Make sure you concentrate solely on the power of each element and don't be judgmental.

How is your navel?

The navel is the center of your power. It really doesn't matter whether your belly is flat or rounded, the crucial thing is how much energy is contained there. The navel represents our center and at the same time is a symbol that what we do is at the center of the universe. In the womb, we were connected to Mother Nature through our navels and this link remains unbroken throughout our lives.

In the past, the Hawaiian people would greet one another with the question: "How's your navel doing?" This meant something like: "Do you have all the energy you need?" A good question! If our center of energy is full, we are ideally placed to put our ideas into practice and to be powerful in our actions. By using our navels, we can tap straight into the elemental forces of Nature and use the inexhaustible source of the universe's power.

Exercise: How it all began

This is a great exercise if you are standing on a mountaintop or beside a stream, or if there is a storm brewing. Imagine how the piece of ground on which you happen to be standing came into being. Let the elemental forces of Nature connect with one another in a wild dance: imagine the sea rising up, volcanoes spewing lava and fragments of rock, the wind blowing from all directions, thunder and lightning raging, and the earth heaving and shaking. As this birth is taking place, welcome it. Don't be afraid; open yourself up to the experience of feeling these elemental forces. Be aware that this elemental power is also within you, that you were made from this primordial soup as well. Catch just a hint of your elemental power, and take it in through your navel.

Ritual: Nourish your power

At the beginning of this book, you read the story of how the love affair between humans and Nature began. Hawaiians see the taro, a variety of yam, as the living manifestation of *Haloa*, the older brother who is the embodiment of Nature. There are all kinds of foodstuffs available to us, but whatever we happen to be eating or drinking, it embodies the power of Nature. Every bite and every sip provides us with energy and gives us strength for what we are about to do. Eating with this attitude has the great advantage that both our stomachs and our power centers will be properly nourished.

Telepathy is easy!

Deep within us, we are aware of this close link with Nature and the primordial power of the elements. We are capable of taking life easy and we have the potential to display our telepathic abilities. Telepathy is not magic, anyone can do it and no particular talent is required. You came into this world with this ability, too. Telepathy is the ideal way of getting in touch with Nature, and is a means of communication that both sides understand. Telepathy is direct, inner communication without the use of spoken or body language. With telepathy, we send and receive messages in the form of thoughts, feelings, symbols, and images, and we can interpret them, too. Telepathy can operate between people, and between people and Nature. Our entire "real" world is permeated by an invisible, subtle substance, the energy field of the universe. This universal energy field reacts with great sensitivity to thoughts, movements, and emotions, and it transfers energy and information. We also have an energetic body, known as an aura or the "subtle body." It constantly changes in form, size, consistency, frequency, and color through our thoughts, feelings, imaginations, and actions. Some people are able to perceive or sense this. When we experience joy at finding the first ripe tomato of the season, the size and brightness of our aura changes immediately. We use the energies of Nature to stimulate our aura, thus raising our energy levels. This has a direct effect on how we put our ideas into practice.

Exercise: Cleanse your antennae

From birth, we are all endowed with powerful feelers in the form of our senses. These "feelers" extend deep into the universal energy field, like antennae that can receive signals. In the most positive sense of the words, we are both receptive and limitless. To dream with Nature and ensure the best possible reception, cleanse, revitalize, and refine your feelers. Imagine the many feelers extending from your body out into the energy field of the universe. Take the first idea that occurs to you and go with it; cleanse, revitalize, and refine these antennae, and enjoy the new, improved reception quality.

Choosing an element

Don't worry about not choosing the right element, simply trust your intuition. You can't make a mistake. You are more intuitive and sensitive than you think. As your connection with the energies of Nature improves, your intuition will awaken, just like Snow White in the fairy tale; you'll trust yourself more and more, and will follow your instincts. There are various ways to find the most suitable element for your purposes:

1. Look around you until something catches your eye; this is the element you're looking for.

2. Number the seven elements from one to seven. Think about what you wish to achieve, and choose the number that your gaze stops on, or take the number that you think of first.

3. Use a dowsing pendulum or a kinesiological muscle test to find the right element.

4. Write the names of the seven elements at random on a sheet of paper. Close your eyes, place your finger over the names on the paper, lower it to point at one, and you've found your element.

5. Take the first thought of an element that comes into your head and try to find a connection with this force of Nature.

6. Choose seven photographs or images, one of each element, and use your intuition to pick one.

7. Orient your thoughts. Let's say you are suffering from backache and are thinking about how good it would be to have something to lean on. Now choose a support from your collection of elements: a tree, a strong bear, or an angel, perhaps. The one that feels best spontaneously will be a great choice.

8. Give free rein to your creativity and find your own way to choose an element.

Techniques for tapping into Nature

Active daydreaming

We are born into this life to give it shape and to be powerful. Whether you're simply fixing lunch or dreaming of leading a self-sufficient life in the country, these are all ideas waiting to be put into practice in the best possible way. When we have an idea, we are playing with different thoughts and scenarios in our head, and we move easily and effortlessly in the realm of the possible. When we daydream or imagine things, we conjure up pictures in our heads, sensual experiences and good feelings. Imagine walking barefoot on the beach, and notice how your body reacts: it creates a sense of relaxation, the soles of your feet feel warm, and you might even taste salt on your tongue; it's exactly the same experience as being at the beach itself.

Active daydreaming means imagining something, picturing it to yourself, and retaining this image in your mind for a short while; in so doing, you are combining deep concentration with a concrete goal—this is a valuable tool for working with the energies of Nature.

If you feel a task is too much for you and you want to look to Nature for help, visualize yourself going about the task in a relaxed fashion, and then let your gaze wander about you. Your eyes may come to rest on the rubber plant in your sitting room, for example, and you can maintain this contact until you feel better. You have linked a concrete goal (relaxation) with concentrating on the rubber plant, and your goal of greater relaxation has become reality. Ideas that become reality are simply a question of energy and application.

The recipe for effortlessly tapping into the energies of Nature might follow this example: take a thought, combine it with pleasant feelings and sensual experience, and add concentration on a particular element. This immediately creates a dynamic and vital recipe and unleashes an unstoppable force. Active daydreaming and/or visualization creates a synthesis of forces in which our needs and the energies of Nature combine. The universe has a solution for everything: Creation has consciously equipped us with the forces of Nature. Let's make use of this wealth of power and richness.

Four ways of tapping into the elemental forces of Nature

Here's where I show you an excellent tool used by the great healers: four different ways in which you can make use of the energies of Nature. It is an approach with significant advantages: you can choose your preferred way, like picking a channel on television. One of the secrets of the great healers is always to choose the way that best reinforces your own strength and the power of your ideas. Here is an example: four people are walking toward a wood.

The first notices the distance to the trees and calculates how long it will take to reach them; for this person the wood is just a waypoint on that day's walk.

The second concentrates on the beautiful color of the trees' foliage and the buzzard hovering over the treetops, feeling the connection with the wood in the powerful steps he is taking. The wood is the source of his power.

The third has connected with the wood and wants to move in silence among the trees and follow his own thoughts. For him, the forest is an oasis, a space for meditation.

The fourth dives straight in at first sight of the wood and forgets all the others around him. He identifies so strongly with woodland that he feels how it feels. For him, the wood is a way of immersing himself in a completely different world.

Each of these people is using the power of the wood in a particular way, a way that is best suited to their personal needs and gives them strength and power. You can play around with these different ways as well.

Take the example described above, and let's suppose you are the first walker. The wood is a waypoint on your hike, which you want to finish at a particular time so you can catch the bus back home. You're running a bit late, you're stressed, and you want to be making progress to reach the bus stop in time. Seen through the eyes of the second walker, you immediately feel more strength and drive, and you can pick up the pace. The third option will help you to find a new direction for your thoughts; the calm of the forest will give you confidence that you will reach your goal. In the fourth option, feeling at one with the wood will help you to put time pressure to the back of your mind and simply be in the moment, just breathing and keeping going.

Each of these options is a way to tap into the elemental forces of the wood, and depending on the situation, one or other will produce the best results. Try it yourself. Here's a general guide to show you the essentials of each option:

Option 1
You focus your attention on the individual components of the bigger picture, analyzing, evaluating, and identifying details. You understand things rationally and intellectually, but you can take action quickly, keeping your distance, recovering from emotional upset, and examining a situation soberly.

Option 2
You tap into the elements of Nature, speak to them, and receive answers. You exchange thoughts, feelings, and images; this is the world of telepathy. You communicate with the beings of Nature, animals and plants, and connect with the forces of Nature.

Option 3
You use the energies of Nature as a symbol. A tree, a shower of rain, or a bird feather can be an omen, a talisman, an object of power, or a sign to do something. Anything you encounter in Nature that catches your attention will be suitable for this; you decide what it means and what support it can give you. In this way, you are intimately connected with the primordial power of the elements.

Option 4

You sense and experience Nature holistically. You are Nature, a tree, a lake, or the wind, and you feel this power within and around you. This is very useful if you are working with the weather, starting something new, or want to discover something new about yourself.

Exercise: Try different options

For this exercise, choose a plant and explore its power in different ways.

- Look closely at the plant, its stalk, its leaves, and flowers. Describe their shape, colors, and size in as much detail as possible.

- Feel your connection with this plant; perceive it as a living being with which you can communicate, a being that is receptive to your thoughts and feelings. Send out loving thoughts to it and imagine receiving a loving thought in return.

- See the plant as a symbol of yourself, of something associated with you, your personality, your dreams, or your preferences. What does it make you think of?

- Imagine yourself getting smaller. Shrink yourself down and squeeze inside the plant. Feel how the plant feels in your position, how it is faring, and what it needs.

Leave the plant, and decide which option you found most pleasant. Linger with this feeling for as long as you like before returning to your daily routine.

Look after yourself

In shamanic cultures there is a rule that I strongly recommend, and that is: "Whatever you do, do it with as much power as possible." However, this is not asking us to simply keep going until we're flat on the floor, so exhausted that we want to extend breaks and rest times for as long as possible; instead, we should take stock every so often and look at how our power reserves are holding out. This has a very positive effect on our condition after completing a task. A small power boost can be extremely effective.

Exercise

As you go about your daily life, always ask yourself the same question: "What element would help me feel powerful now?" Trust your intuition and take the first thought that comes into your head. There are many possible starting points for interpreting our thoughts; we just have to "read between the lines." If you are seeking more power right now, let a mighty fall wind fill your sails. If you are feeling very cold and tired, wrap yourself in a sunshine coat. If you feel listless and unable to concentrate, picture yourself under a waterfall. Do whatever occurs to you on the spur of the moment. This is a very simple and highly effective way to stay powerful.

Techniques for communicating with Nature

Good vibrations

"I'm picking up good vibrations," as it says in the old song from the 60s. Make sure you are, too. Nature is just like us: it likes to be treated with respect, to be approached with an open heart and with care. Our energy fields will then come into harmony with one another and our intuitive perception will be enhanced. Here are some suggestions for ways to ensure good vibrations.

I'm ready!

Be accessible, open up every cell in your body, spread out your energy field to demonstrate your readiness to invite the energies of Nature into every cell of your being. You will be at the helm, directing this power; it will follow your instructions and nothing will happen unless you want it to.

Make sure you are on the same wavelength

Research into the way people communicate tells us that those who use similar words, gestures, and body language understand one another better and establish a connection with each other more quickly. It's no different when you communicate with Nature. The natural elements are filled with dynamic and precious power that they love to use. They are intensely and vitally active for every second of their existence. You will communicate with them more easily if you seek contact with joyful expectation and a desire for action. Both your energy fields will then have the same frequency, immediately creating a feeling of intimacy and enabling information to flow back and forth much more effortlessly.

A clear direction

What do you want? What kind of support do you need? What should Nature help you with? Nature can best use its powers if you have clear goals, made clearer by a positive visualization of the outcome. For example, perhaps you are hoping for a good day's hiking without getting soaked? Then express a clear ambition (dry conditions for your hike), visualize a positive outcome (a gap in the clouds gathering stubbornly over the area where you are hiking, an enjoyable place for lunch in the open air, clouds that scud away quickly), and add a little gratitude and joy for the support. This is the way to achieve the best results. The energies of Nature like things to be precise, clear, and direct.

Listen carefully

The messages the elements send to one or other of our senses often take unconventional routes. Listening carefully and paying attention allows us to recognize and take in even the smallest and most fleeting of messages. Being able to wait, and enjoy waiting, is a very special quality and helps us to be present in the moment. Sometimes the communication will come as the proverbial thunderclap, but at other times it will just be a gentle caress. The elements are wise; follow their lead and their prompting. Turn off your head and turn on your intuition!

Show yourself

Nature has faith in us. It assumes that we will make active use of the powerful gifts it gives us, bringing dynamism to stagnant situations, taking bold action and the next small step in our personal development. There is no giving up in Nature; it is always in motion, and seizes every opportunity. The best way to thank Nature for its support is by following its example and doing our very best, staying watchful, and making the most of even the smallest of opportunities.

Energy is never wasted with the elements; they seek the path of least resistance, and the more connected we are with Nature, the more easily and smoothly we will deal with life. We'll learn to apply our strengths more effectively, become more decisive and resilient, and have the courage to stick at even large-scale projects over the long term. A tiny delicate flower or a mighty active volcano: both are powerful and good at what they do. They don't hide themselves away, they show their individual strength. In Nature it is not a question of being big or small, but rather of expressing all your strength and not hiding away in a corner. This is self-confidence par excellence and a good example to follow.

Give praise and appreciation

We are all happy to receive a little praise or appreciation, and it's the same with Nature. Each element is useful and important in its way. Praise the many good things that the energies of Nature achieve, and make this the basis for heart-to-heart communication. A little whisper of gratitude while out walking, as you clean the yard, while you're preparing food, or driving will strengthen the thin beam of light that connects you to Nature. Gifts are always welcome (in shamanic cultures people offer tobacco or maize, for example). Nourishing plants with fertilizer made from stinging nettles, allowing the soil time to recuperate before sowing the next crop, watering, choosing a product with less wasteful packaging at the store. Nature loves gifts like these, and will work all the more happily with us.

But you don't have to get too serious about it. You can still laugh about things; for example, there's no need to get annoyed if the wind disturbs the pile of leaves you have just swept up—enjoy the joke with the elements and show you can laugh. I have no doubt that the energies of Nature have a great sense of humor, watching with a twinkle in the eye as they see what we and the other elements get up to. The elements are not striving for perfection; they are working toward harmonic coexistence and asking us to enjoy life!

Exercise: A greetings ritual

I often do this ritual when I am outside in Nature, whether I'm jogging, digging up weeds, or cycling to the store. I inhale the forces that surround me with every breath and become more energized. Then I open up every cell in my body and extend my energy field far beyond myself, greeting everything around me with thanks. I caress every blade of grass, bug, and stone with my aura; they are part of my family. I breathe in deeply through my navel and open my senses to the scents, colors, sounds, and fragrances of Nature. This is my way of giving thanks continually and expressing my appreciation. This ritual brings me an immediate feeling of wellbeing and great strength. Devise a greeting ritual that works for you.

Exercise: A gratitude ritual

I like things to be simple but at the same time highly effective, something that is equally true of my favorite gratitude ritual. I thought of it on the spur of the moment many years ago and it has much appeal. When I achieve something, I am glad and appreciative, and I have learned something new. I imagine to myself that, in doing this, I gain an inner or outer beauty and radiance, either visibly or invisibly, and so I concentrate on something beautiful nearby and devote myself entirely to this beauty for a minute or two. It might be a force of Nature, but any object or person can embody Nature as well; we have an entirely free choice. I then try to perceive this beauty in its entirety and explore every aspect of it.

Everything in the universe is beautiful in its own individual and very particular way; it is beautiful as it has come from Nature. By honoring beauty, I pay homage to Nature, the beauty within all living things, and the beauty within me. This short and simple ritual lights a beacon of gratitude and makes our world an even more beautiful place.

How to communicate with the elemental forces of Nature

- Think of an element of Nature and send out a thin beam of light through the universe's energy field to that element.
- The more intensely you concentrate on the element, the more powerful this thin beam of light will be. Actually touching or feeling the forces of Nature may help to support you as you focus.

- You can now send out your request and receive the energy of the forces of Nature.
- The brighter your beam of light and the more energy it contains, the better your reception will be among the elements, and the more you will feel.
- This light connection will continue for as long as you wish, and will become stronger with each elemental contact.
- You will have especially strong light connection to parts of Nature that you like and respect, or elements with which you associate pleasant experiences.

Exercise: Perceive a beam of light

Choose something in Nature, such as a tree or an animal, or a lake or the sunlight, and sit in front of it or look out at it, and imagine a beam of light stretching from your navel to your chosen piece of Nature. Reinforce this beam of light by praising all the things that make this part of Nature special.

Exercise: Receive answers from a stone

Pick up a stone and hold it in your hand. Be aware that this stone has an energetic body and that you are connected to one another by a beam of light; the connection is made as soon as you pick up the stone. You can decide what information you wish to send to the stone, and request answers from it. The link between you will become stronger with every contact. The more joy, curiosity, and trust that accompanies your communications, the stronger your sensations will be. You will then be able to connect with the stone and exploit its power simply by calling it to mind.

To round off this chapter, I'd like to pique your curiosity and enthusiasm for other practical applications with a short Irish tale.

One time while I was on vacation in Ireland, I spent a day on the Burren, a treeless, stony landscape whose charm lies in its barrenness.

While looking for a hiking trail, I bumped into a man called Ian, who was searching for his cows. We walked part of the way together and he invited me to join him in visiting a spring. Ian knew the area like the back of his hand.

We were talking about my work when Ian suddenly suggested that he show me a very special place. He was interested in making ecological use of the natural resources. He wanted to clear an area that was covered in shrubs, fully aware that they would grow back in no time, and use them as fuel for heating. But he didn't want to do this without permission from the elemental beings living there.

Eager for some adventure, I accompanied Ian to his special place, which we reached in around an hour. Once there, I opened myself up to it completely, extended my aura, made contact with the elementals, and invited them to show themselves. There were several "leaders," and it was to them that I set out Ian's concerns in thoughts and images. They showed me a very magical place and asked me to leave everything as it was there; they said it was their meeting place and that it also acted as a kind of magnet for elemental beings from other areas.

Ian smiled and said that he always got goosebumps at this spot. He asked if there was anything else he should bear in mind, and whether the noise and the disturbance of the work would trouble the elemental beings? But they smiled and told him that they would support his plan in their way. What was important to them was to be included and to recognize that there was a good intention behind the whole undertaking.

After this successful encounter, Ian had another request. We walked to a ramshackle shepherd's hut. This hut had once been used by English officials collecting rent and taxes for the landlords, generally a thankless task since the Irish didn't like them and the officials would much rather have stayed at home. Ian told me that he felt sad for a moment whenever he passed by the hut.

We climbed up on to the roof together and I called to the spirit of the hut, a hobgoblin, in my thoughts. It appeared to me, gagged and in handcuffs. Symbolically, its appearance represented oppression and the loss of liberty. I invited Ian to free the spirit and to call upon the elemental beings of the area to bring that place back to life and develop a new way of coexisting. Ian and I parted, happily and spiritually nourished.

TAKING PRACTICAL STEPS: THE ENERGIES OF NATURE IN YOUR DAILY ROUTINE

This type of support and healing work is extremely diverse—I can assure you that you won't get bored—there is no such thing as monotony in Nature. We have a wide range of needs in our daily lives, whether it's taking an afternoon off work, doing the housework, or having a conversation to resolve a situation. The reason we are on this Earth is to become ever better at making use of our natural connections in order to implement these needs. The more energy we have, the more effective we are. We have good tools at our disposal, we have become acquainted with the elements, and we have set up a power circle. Living naturally is really energizing; having "lit the blue touch paper," we will no longer be content with just sparklers!

I will now explain a range of alternative options. For the sake of simplicity, each exercise will mostly concentrate on one element. You are not restricted to this, however, and can do the exercises with another element whenever you like. There are of course plenty of real-life accounts from course participants or my own experience; these are powerful and inspiring stories that will only serve to strengthen our desire to smoothly integrate the energies of Nature into our daily lives.

Tapping into the energies of Nature through meditation

When we meditate we are in a state of concentrated attentiveness. We focus on something and maintain our concentration. Most people are able to concentrate on something comfortably for about six seconds. When we can maintain our focus for a minute, we are meditating; this is long enough to energize the object of our concentration and to direct it, together with a force of Nature, along the right path. We can use these units of a minute for the same issue, and turn a desire or wish into a magnet for benevolent forces, or integrate a force of Nature into what we are already doing. Briefly imagining that there is a crackling fire burning in our navels is more than enough to achieve this; we have already tapped into the power of fire and can get on with our work with more dynamism. The more relaxed we are, the better we are, and the more closely we feel the power of our work with the elements. In this respect, it is good to remember that there is no unnatural tension in Nature; integrating the elements has the positive side effect that we relax and are better able to concentrate on the power of Nature. Finding a focus and combining it with the energies of Nature can turn a weak ray of sunlight trying to find its way through the mist into the blazing intensity of the sun at midday.

Combining daily activities with the energies of Nature

Combine your routine activities with the elemental forces of Nature in this very simple way and you will find you have greater strength for them. Here are a few examples drawn from real life:

Rocks + walking: The bones of the Earth are like coiled springs giving power to my legs. With this thought in mind I am able to walk with agility for hours, and above all, keep up with my husband.

Plants + self-confidence: I stroll past several cornfields during the summer. As soon as the first stalks appear, I walk down a row and imagine that they are lining up for me, applauding and waving to me in complete admiration. When the corn is about hip-high, I walk along the side of the field, imagining the same thing. I don't think you can have too much self-confidence!

Water + medicine: I have got into the habit of making my own healing water. I add to the water either homeopathic pellets, a slice of lemon, Schuessler tissue salts, or good thoughts. With every sip, I bring to mind the "ingredients" and the "desired outcome"; it has given drinking water a whole new meaning.

Fire + cycling: When cycling in the heat of the summer, I think to myself "Full steam ahead!" I imagine the warmth of the sun as a motor powering my wheels, which allows me to focus on my performance.

Water + cleaning my teeth: I task the water with cleaning and rinsing my teeth especially carefully so that no plaque can build up.

Flying + dandelions: When I first flew with my nephew, he picked a dandelion before getting into the small propeller plane. He held it tightly in his hand throughout the flight. Using the plant's pioneering spirit, he enjoyed every little bit of turbulence and found great joy in flying.

Wind + voice: If I am giving a talk or just generally have the feeling that my voice is not very strong, I let the wind blow into my throat. It clears away everything so that I can express myself properly.

Animal + change of perspective: If I can't think of a solution to a problem, I imagine seeing it through the eyes of another: from the perspective of an eagle or through the eyes of an owl, while the senses of a bat have also often helped me in the past.

We love to eat, and eating is an important part of our daily routine. Cooking, baking, and eating are all good opportunities for using the energies of Nature. Here are four suggestions to try when preparing food. In this scenario you are cutting up slices of apple to eat raw or to include in a pie. You want to go into a scheduled meeting with the power of the apple by your side and inspire the people at the meeting to be enthusiastic about your ideas. Just play around with these options and use them to develop your own strategies.

1st option

As you're chopping the fruit, think about the characteristics of an apple or an apple tree, which could be useful to you right now; people love to see the blossom on an apple tree and its abundance of ripe fruit. As summer progresses, the blossom develops into tasty apples, and the buds for new growth can be seen as early as the fall. Apples contain plenty of vitamin C, boost our immune systems, and thereby also reinforce our enthusiasm for our ideas. You can combine this rational analysis with the power of the apple and simply choose the elements that are useful for whatever your goal; you might like to attend your meeting mentally swathed in a cloak of blossom.

2nd option

Just imagine, simply by touching and preparing it, that you are creating a powerful connection with this apple. Its power is immediately available to you and your energy levels and enthusiasm for the meeting are increasing with every bite. How does this power feel in your body?

3rd option

You can also think of the apple as a symbol and create a link with what you wish to do. Keeping an apple pip in your pocket might symbolically represent your unflagging enthusiasm in the meeting, for example.

4th option

Become one with the apple as you prepare it. Imagine you are the apple: make yourself very small and slip into the apple, or imagine the fruit within you, and allow it to spread out through your whole body. Sense how powerful it feels when you are a plant and present your ideas at the meeting using this power.

5th option

When preparing food, it's easy to introduce action and movement to the mix. Whatever natural element you're working with, you can touch it, smell it, taste it, listen to the sounds it makes, and examine it from every angle.

Depending on the element, you might also rest against it, climb onto it, breathe it in, move around it, or even make something from it. Try whatever you occurs to you. How do you perceive the power of the plant in this way?

These alternative ways of making a conscious connection can be used for every element and every requirement. The following also work very well: stand in water, turn your face to the wind, let the sun shine down on you, hold a stone in your hand, stroke an animal, or observe a creature of Nature.

6th option: Burning incense
Burning incense is traditional in many cultures. It incorporates every element: wind, which scattered the seeds of the incense plants; fire, which lit the incense; water, which kept the plants hydrated; stones in the soil, which nourished the plants; bees, worms, and moles, which pollinated and looked after the soil; while elemental beings did their best to make sure that the incense plants grew healthily. Play around with thoughts in your mind and think a desire through to its fulfillment while burning incense on this mental journey. You could even burn incense that you have found yourself.

7th option: Dealing with obstacles
It is easy to identify the subtle influences to which a plant has been exposed from its external appearance. You have no doubt noticed trees with forked or twisted branches, or strange lumps and bumps. When you see such features, you can assume that the trees are growing over watercourses, fault lines, or other energetic constructs that are not right for them. The trees look for solutions to this kind of disharmony by moving away or twisting and turning. Look out for one of these trees and examine it closely. Your task is to learn how the tree deals with obstacles and other unfavorable conditions. How can you apply what you have learned to your current situation? Alternatively, use any other element to learn how it deals with resistance and obstacles. Look at the wind buffeting the side of houses, watch fish swimming in an aquarium, or see how sunlight is obscured by clouds.

Real-life accounts

Ria

I really like doing the meditation "Dealing with Obstacles" using water. I live quite close to a river where there is a large dam. I stand beside the dam and look at the river. I want to learn more about how the river deals with the obstacle. Does the dam paralyze the river, is the river overawed by it, does the water fight with the dam wall? At the moment, I have the feeling that I am standing in my own way. I have dreams but I never get myself in gear to do anything about them. This is the issue I think about when I stand at the dam.

The first thing that strikes me is that the river is always in motion. Although there's no wind today, the water flows continually and tirelessly toward the wall; it looks like it will never give up. It has chosen a direction and is following this focus. I direct all my concentration on the area where the water meets the wall. Is there a struggle taking place here? It doesn't appear so. It's more as though they are playing together in a game of strength, giving in to circumstances.

I walk another few steps and watch how the water flows from an open sluice gate. It reminds me of children screaming for joy as they go down a slide. The urge for the water to plunge down deep is obvious and I feel joy and a desire to follow its example. Thank you, water, for teaching me this.

Lydia

I'm a child of the sun and I can't get enough warmth. That said, I am also very reserved. This isn't especially helpful for me in my everyday life and I would like to open up more. For me, the sun is the symbol of showing yourself. So what symbolic power does the sun have for me? To answer *this question, I sat out on my balcony in the sun, consciously opened my eyes, and looked up at the sunshine. At first I was blinded. Aha, I don't like people who try to dazzle me: is that why I hide my light under a bushel? It could be! The sun has many rays and it shows many aspects of itself. How many aspects of myself would I like to show in public? It's a good question; I'll think about it.*

How exciting would it be to tell people that I'm a woman and I can use a battery-powered drill and change from summer to winter tires myself, that I like romantic poems and go on protest marches from time to time? That wouldn't be an issue for the sun. The longer I sit here, the more I sense the sun and the better I feel. I would get the same sense of wellbeing if I were to put myself in the spotlight.

Suddenly a cloud appears and partially covers the sun. Okay, it can deal with other elements being nearby; it waits until the cloud moves away or pushes it to one side. I can do that too, when I've had enough of the spotlight; I can take a step back. It was an exciting symbolic exchange: the sun is now my symbol for showing more of myself.

Marcus

I really enjoy the meditation options. By nature, I like to analyze things, so I'm more of a reason-based person. I was taking a meditative stroll one Sunday morning. I had read that nomads have a completely different relationship with Nature: when they walk over stones, they become the stone, and they concentrate all their attention on this. I wanted to try it, and walked along country paths for half an hour; I wanted to try out the various meditation options. First, I walked for a few minutes and just took in the different shapes of the stones. Then I concentrated on feeling the effect the stones were having on the soles of my feet and listening to the sound as my shoes and the stones met.

After a while, I started to look for a stone to bring balance; I wanted to find one that looked as much like an equilateral triangle as possible. It took me quite some time, but I eventually picked one up and imagined what it would be like to be this stone. Each of the options had impressed me in its own way, and I was able to involve my analytic abilities. I liked the second option the best on this occasion; I felt the connection to the power of the stones most powerfully.

Tapping into the spirits of the elements

Just as you can work with the material manifestation of an element, you can also work with its spirit. What is the spirit of an element, the spirit of water, of animals, or of fire? Its spirit is its subtle nature, its essence, its essential power, and the invisible creative force that lurks beneath the visible element. Spiritual beings are living power packs full of dynamism and wisdom. Everything in Nature is full of life, has a spirit, and is ready to work with us.

A Mongolian nomad woman once told me: "Spirits are good energies that live within the elements as power. Look at the steppes, how full of life and vital and adaptable they are; you are connected to this energy. That is the spirit of the steppes. It's the same with the spirit of water, of fire, or of an animal. Each thing has its own individual characteristic energy." We cannot see spirit beings in the conventional way, as they have a different vibration, but when we engage with them with childlike curiosity, we recognize them as pulsing energy fields, moving in every direction, showing themselves in a way we can perceive. Spirit beings possess only an energetic body, whereas humans have a physical body as well.

What abilities do they have?

Spirit beings are great healers and lively personalities. They understand us completely, influencing our subtle bodies, and are honest, clear, and rational; they address issues directly. They can see through things and can read our thoughts. The spirit of the elements can penetrate anywhere, through anything.

These spirit beings have the ability to heal, to inspire, bring harmony, boost our essential strength, or to do whatever is necessary to solve a problem or meet a need. When we connect with an element, we tap into the invisible power that is inherent within it: the spirit of plants is the power that brings forth fruit and branches, and the spirit of water shapes liquid into raindrops, hailstones, or snowflakes. Every element has its own rhythm, its own individual qualities and, depending on the time and circumstances, will offer a different form of support. There is a wealth of powers to choose from and we can select our ideal partner. If we can't make the decision ourself, we can intuitively hand it over to Nature; in its wisdom, Nature will show us which source of power would be ideal at any precise moment. For the following exercises, you might like to go outside into Nature or to sit in your power circle.

Exercise: Get to know all the spirits

Begin by inviting the spirit of the wind to show itself. There are many ways to perceive it: through your thoughts, through physical reactions, or through sight or sound. Maintain contact for as long as you wish, then call on the spirits of the other elements, one after another.

Exercise: Healing work with the spirit of the elements

Choose something that you would like to have or improve connected with your body. Do you dream of thicker hair, better digestion, or a more flexible spine? Wait a while and see which spirit being presents itself to you. How does it show itself? Allow this spirit to work with, and within, your body and to have a healing effect.

Exercise: The spirits' dance of freedom

We all want to be seen as whole human beings and not just to be perceived superficially as a perfect housewife, for example, or a patient listener or talented computer expert. When we meet with elemental spirits, we will be viewed holistically. These spirit beings will help us to be more ourselves; then we can look beyond the facade, behind the protective screens, and recognize our own true power, our actual potential to shape our own lives. Invite the elemental spirits to show your true nature, little by little. Watch and enjoy the spirits' dance of freedom. This ritual is equally wonderful by the light of a full moon.

Exercise: Good things come in threes

Sixteenth-century physician and alchemist Paracelsus recognized long ago that there are three things that work together to produce a remedy: substance, energy, and spirit. Think about this when you drink a glass of water. As you do so you are introducing water into your body, you are receiving an energy boost from the liquid, and you can tell the spirit of water what healing effect you would like to receive. You're killing three birds with one stone!

Exercise: Increase harmony

Think of an issue concerning you that is connected with the idea of protection and choose an elemental spirit. When we need protection, it is because there is disharmony between our energy field and that of another person. Invite the spirit to harmonize both energy fields so that you feel powerful.

Exercise: Adaptation

The elements are masters of adaptation. Desert plants, upland moors, camels, all the manifestations of water: these are just a few examples of the enormous adaptability of the elements. If you are experiencing a lot of change in your life at the moment, but your instant reaction is that you don't like it, call upon a spirit being and be inspired by the concept of adaptation.

Exercise: The spirit of a stone tells a story

Select a stone and let it tell you a story. Take one that you have had for some time, or choose a stone from the path in front of your house. Pick a dream that you want to become reality, and listen carefully to the stone to find out how it can come true. Rocks are superb storytellers. Just try it!

Exercise: Become a spirit being

Would you like to go wild, like a fire spirit, or find out more about the life of a water spirit? Become the spirit of an element: slip inside its skin and experience the world from its perspective. Observe the effect it has on your body, your feelings, and your thoughts.

Exercise: Healing properties

Make use of the healing pharmacy of Nature. The healers of the past knew all about the healing power of herbs, even though they had no equipment or laboratories; they spoke to the spirits of the plants. Do you enjoy tomatoes with basil, chive bread, or pepper steaks? Then ask the spirits of these plants about their healing properties.

Exercise: Feel beautiful

"Mirror, mirror, on the wall, who is the fairest of them all?" Every day, we all wonder how we look. The elements bring beauty to light and stimulate our aesthetic sensitivity. The elements can point the way to ourselves. Each element is true to itself and lives only in its own way; no plant wants to be the wind, and no fire has ambitions to be an animal. The elements know what they have to do, and how to do it. Communicating with the spirits of the elements is like conducting an inner dialogue, and the spirits can help us get to know ourselves better. They will take us along a magical path to inner beauty and strength. Meet with the spirit of an element and imagine looking in its mirror. What do you see? What form of beauty is reflected back at you? What beautiful aspects of you does it bring out?

Exercise: Dream with plant spirits

In some cultures people believe it is the spirit of a plant that brings about healing. They recommend inviting the spirit of the plant into our nightly dreams, or meeting with it and making it a part of our desire for healing. When using herbal medicine, you can boost its effects by meeting the plant's spirit; it will make your medicine strong, embodying a powerful dream. You can also ask the spirit of the plant to include you in its own dreams.

Real-life accounts

Lara

The "feeling beautiful" ritual caught my attention straight away. I looked into the stone spirit's mirror. I perceive the stone spirit as a great being, clad in colors ranging from light blue to dark gray. Its face is quite fierce and it moves very slowly, shuffling and yet somehow also with elegance. The mirror that I looked into was at least as big as me, with an ornate silver frame. Looking back at me from the mirror was a little girl with blond curls and a little pink dress; she reminded me of my daughter. It could be that I haven't felt beautiful since she was born. All at once, I felt an impulse to destroy this image. It was really easy, and then I saw myself as much larger than in real life, and I was radiating a power and presence that put everything else in the shade. All the things I found wrong with my body were suddenly no longer important; I saw myself as I really was, a strong woman. I give myself this image as a gift every morning when I look in the mirror.

Gill

I haven't had much practice in visualizing or seeing images, which is why I use my pendulum when I wish to know which elemental spirit will be useful for what I want to do. I have laid out a picture for each element and numbered these images in order. I recite the numbers from one to seven in my head and see when the pendulum moves; I then connect with that element.

Achim

I had been thinking long and hard about how I was going to deal with the fact that my son is continually being tormented by two other boys in kindergarten. I had a few ideas, but I wasn't sure which was the best strategy. I went into the garden and asked the spirit of the wind for advice. The answer came into my head very quickly: "I don't decide what moves. I blow and blow, and change direction according to circumstances." That sounds meaningful to me and a challenge to get started with something; I won't get anything done if I just think about it, and if that is not working, I shall change my approach.

Alexa

I'm really not happy with this year's crop of gherkins for pickling, although I didn't do anything different from previous years. I thought I would ask the wild herbs, and I chose the spirit of the dandelion: it's a plant that grows everywhere, even in the most difficult conditions. I see the plant spirit as a kind of soil doctor who first runs a few crumbs of earth through *his fingers and sniffs them before finally placing a few in his mouth and chewing on them. But he doesn't pull a face; he moves the crumbs of earth around in his mouth, like a wine connoisseur with a sip of wine, concentrating hard. I watch, getting slightly impatient, and wait. Then the plant doctor nods, searches in his trouser pocket and brings out a worm. I wait, but there are no other worms to follow. So my soil needs more of these useful little fellows. I shall hedge my bets, meet up with the worm spirit, and find out how I can bring my garden soil back to life.*

Frida

I read an article about polar bears and I couldn't stop thinking about them. I decided to meet the spirit of the polar bear to find out what advice it would give me for healing a badly swollen mosquito bite. I perceived the spirit as a white fountain, spurting upward and then subsiding, rising and subsiding; nothing else happened. Without thinking too much about it, I placed this vision in the center of the mosquito bite and waited. I didn't think much more about it over the course of the day, but by the evening, the swelling had indeed gone down.

Suzanne

A Hawaiian healer who came from a long line of healers told me the following story about rocks. Her great-grandmother would go on long walks to the top of the highest mountain, where she gathered small black rocks by the light of the full moon. Having returned home, she placed the rocks in a bowl of water and put it by the window. She changed the water every day, and one day discovered that the rocks had had little babies. These original rocks have since been handed down from generation to generation and they have continually given birth to more rocks. These are used as medicines; a really strong rock spirit must live within them.

Tapping into elemental beings

"When the first baby laughed for the first time, its laugh broke into a thousand pieces, and they all went skipping about, and that was the beginning of fairies. When a new baby laughs for the first time a new fairy is born, and as there are always new babies there are always new fairies." *Peter Pan* by J. M. Barrie.

The energy field of the universe is in motion all around us. It is also the home of the elemental beings of Nature. They are much subtler than us, and Nature is full of such beings. Fairies, dwarves, elves, gnomes, and kobolds share this life with us and their stories and adventures have spoken to us since our childhood. There's the little mermaid, the tooth fairy, Tinkerbell, and Dobby the house elf in Harry Potter, not to mention hobbits; and supernatural characters even crop up in Shakespeare's *A Midsummer Night's Dream*.

We are endlessly fascinated by these beings. Have you too dreamed of getting in touch with them? Now you can! In Iceland, there is reportedly an "elf lobby" that is consulted when streets or building developments are planned. More than half of the Icelanders believe in elves and want to maintain good relations with their invisible fellow inhabitants. Ireland is another country that sets great store by a good relationship with its elemental beings; the Irish talk of the "little people," who have incredible abilities, penetrating the Earth with a glance and making beautiful music. Elemental beings have their own intelligence and wisdom. They tell good stories and give wise advice—being in contact with them is great fun. It is easy to use our telepathic abilities to talk to dwarves, or we can visit with hobbits, eavesdrop on elves, learn from gnomes, and develop our primordial perception of these beings and make their powers our own.

Types of elemental beings

To make it easier for you to enter the world of elemental beings, let me introduce you to them. Elemental beings are clothed in energy. Do they look like us? It's possible: we see them through the lens of our own preconceptions, of course. Elemental beings can be tiny or large, thin or fat, transparent or extremely colorful, clothed or naked; they might wear little caps or scarves, have perky wings or a sagging bosom, be blond or dark-haired, and live alone or in groups. These small people have great power, however.

Each elemental being has a particular role in the vital processes of Nature. They shape, change, clean, inspire, open doors, and whirl around the place. They take care of everything in Nature and never cause harm, but they have a sense of humor and often get up to mischief, although they are never malicious.

Dwarves

Dwarves are a people of small stature. They live in nooks and crannies deep in the bowels of the Earth and have immense powers. They work with minerals and have great knowledge of healing crystals. They usually wear pointed caps and long beards, and are are already fully grown by the age of three. Dwarves, gnomes, trolls, and goblins are all from the same family and look very alike. Some are gnarled, wrinkled, and slightly mushroom-shaped, resembling a tree root, while others are muscular, with red cheeks and large hands and feet.

Goblins and kobolds, and pixies

I am always reminded of Samuel Taylor Coleridge's poem, which begins:

> *Whom the untaught Shepherds call*
> *Pixies in their madrigal.*
> *Fancy's children, here we dwell:*
> *Welcome, Ladies! to our cell.*

Did you love pixies as a child, as I did? One of mine is with me still and is standing on my desk. They are the protectors of the house and are said to like living under thresholds, cupboards, and floorboards, or tucked away in nooks and crannies. They often have disheveled hair and flashing eyes, and are very quick and nimble. They have a good sense of humor and get up to all kinds of mischief. You have probably already encountered the sock pixie; you know he's been around when you can only find one sock. He usually brings it back fairly soon, which is why you can't believe your eyes when the sock turns up in the exact spot where you've already looked three times.

Fairies and elves

Fairies and elves are light-beings: they manifest themselves as airy, transparent, and delicate creatures. Their gossamer wings embody the effortless ease with which they float through life. They radiate wisdom, inspiration, and cheer; it is said that they can absorb the light of the sun and reflect it out into the world. They love sunshine and nights of the full moon, and their magical gifts are available to everyone. They cast spells and enchant both Nature and humans. Fairies and elves possess talismans with magical properties, which they like to give to us.

Nixies and water sprites

Nixies, undines, nymphs, mermaids, and water sprites make their homes in all kinds of water, whether it's the wide ocean, a broad river, a fresh spring, or a tiny pond: this is where they live and where their influence is felt. Female water spirits have been described as bewitchingly beautiful, graceful, and scintillating, with flowing hair and beautiful eyes. Water sprites are said to have hair of matted algae, and are slimy and scaly, and a little clumsy. But don't pay too much attention to these clichés; I have seen some very delicate and wise water sprites. They dance through the water gracefully and speedily and can take many forms.

So, the nature spirits include dwarves, elves, trolls, water sprites, nixies, nymphs, undines, leprechauns, brownies, goblins, pixies, ice giants, kobolds, gnomes, divine messengers, sylphs, dryads, devas, salamanders: the list is endless and is certainly not yet complete. These are just names and decriptive terms that are used to try and separate nature spirits into different categories. But is that even possible? You can decide for yourself which of the nature spirits you encounter. Be glad of such meetings and accept their support for your dreams, both great and small. Nature spirits have fascinated us for centuries; they embody our yearning for a safe and secure world without cares and for people who stand by us, for the magic of the seemingly impossible, and for our invisible friends from childhood. Fortunately, the nature spirits have not deserted us. We just need to allow ourselves to see them.

Exercise: Fairy plants

Fairies are said to like bluebells, foxgloves, wood sorrel, daisies, and columbine in particular; so begin by trying your luck with one of these flowers and meet your first flower fairy. Tell it about one of your dreams.

Exercise: Nature spirits in your power circle

Your power circle of the elements is home to a wealth of nature spirits: it's where you'll meet gnomes, elves, goblins, fairies, and kobolds. Each will be glad to work with you; whatever is troubling you or whatever you wish to do, the appropriate nature spirit is there to help. Try it for yourself.

Exercise: Small creatures with extraordinary powers

Elves, nixies, or gnomes: these small beings all have magical powers and can achieve miracles overnight. What challenging task might these amazing creatures achieve for you in just one night of a full moon?

Exercise: Laugh out loud

How do you like being tickled? It stimulates the energy, activates the immune system, and is also great fun! Invite a cheery gnome, kobold, or goblin to sit beside you on a garden bench, and let the fun begin.

Exercise: Get to know your housemates

We usually go into the garden if we want to see fairies or goblins, but there are plenty of invisible beings living in our homes as well. Get to know your housemates: they are just waiting to help make your house tidier, more energetic, or more inviting. I have a fantastic cleaning goblin who is a great help with spring-cleaning and I also have a pixie for my computer, he dusts and cleans with a tiny little brush, and also makes sure that my computer keeps working.

Exercise: The healing power of rocks

There is a wealth of minerals and stones in the ground. They were created in the bowels of the Earth millions of years ago and have special healing powers. To discover which mineral is best suited to whatever you wish to achieve, ask the dwarves, gnomes, and trolls who specialize in these elements. Choose a good piece of earth, and take your desire for healing deep into the soil to find your rock and minerals specialist.

Exercise: Relax by the water

This exercise is good to carry out beside a lake or riverbank, although placing a small bowl of water in front of you will work, too. Relax as you watch the water sprites and nixies dance. I have also had really good experiences watching the fire elves in the flame of a candle.

Real-life accounts

Ella
"Ring-a ring o' roses, a pocket full of posies, Atishoo, Atishoo, we all fall down."

I've known this magic incantation since I was in kindergarten. We were told that Mother Hulda lived under the elderberry bush and that she had magical powers. You could give the bush anything and it would disappear into its roots. In Grimm's fairy tale about Mother Hulda things fall into the well and emerge completely transformed. This has become a ritual for me, and every time I see an an elderberry bush, I leave something behind. Mother Hulda will know what to do with it. It took time for me to see her properly, but she revealed herself as a beaming, healthy, buxom, well-built woman, always on the move, shaking out her apron, humming a tune, and giving me a wave.

Suzanne
Summer solstice in the plant kingdom
At a summer solstice garden seminar we ended our visit with a trip to the great feast of the Nature spirits. Each participant had already befriended a Nature spirit and asked if they could invite them to the event. It was like a huge celebratory party. Thousands of different Nature spirits attended and there was a dance floor, acrobats, mime artists, jumping competitions, and much more. We all stared in amazement.

Many of the elves and fairies were very smartly dressed and were the queens of the ball. There had been no contest to choose them, each had been allowed to decide for herself. I found some of the small floral gentlemen particularly charming and named them "butler goblins." They looked so formal and distinguished, and when no one was looking they pulled funny faces and made contortions. I was very impressed by the way the Nature spirits interacted with one another; despite the noise and sheer volume of those attending, the atmosphere was so relaxed and cheerful. Everybody did exactly what they felt like doing but got along just fine; it seems society can work without rules and laws.

Harry

My first encounter with the Nature spirits that live beneath the Earth made a huge impression on me. I met a root-gnome who had made his home among the roots of a pink phlox. He didn't live there alone but with several members of his family, and each relative was responsible for a different section of the roots. They dutifully made sure that all the small clods of earth were broken up so that the tiny root hairs had sufficient space and access to water.

When he took a brief break to catch his breath, I was able to observe him a little more closely. He had large, friendly eyes and very warm hands, which he laid on my chest. Energy streamed through my torso, giving me the feeling that I could breathe freely again. Since my divorce I have felt a tightness in my chest and I was astonished at how this root-gnome intuitively knew what I needed. To show my gratitude, I planted a pink phlox just like his in my garden.

Marla

I first saw Nature spirits during a Nature seminar. I was really motivated and went home, sat down on the terrace, and waited, full of curiosity to know if there was anything to see here as well. As if by magic, I was imme-diately drawn to the corner where I store my compost. In the undergrowth behind it was an absolute riot of Nature spirits. A small fairy invited me to have a look around her home, a small delicate house made of green light. Her elf friends had just come to visit and were making music together. You might think I'm crazy, but I really did hear a melody and hummed along to it. I found it so moving that tears ran down my face. I now see this corner of my garden with a new pair of eyes, and I often go there and tell the small fairy about my dream of being completely healthy again, and ask her for help; the small fairy has prescribed so many pretty melodies for me already.

Chrissie

I love it when the dandelions bloom in spring, and I wanted to get to know the invisible helpers who ensure that these flowers are so bright and beautiful. I met a tiny light-being that I named Light Elf. It wasn't easy to make this creature out, she was just a faint outline of blue light, but she was wearing a cute little hat and had slightly pointed ears. She had a tiny brush with her, and was carefully cleaning and polishing each petal. Every so often she would rearrange a petal that had got out of place. She barely had time to acknowledge me, she was so lost in her work, but it was enough for me simply to observe this busy little elf and to share her joy in her task. Infected with her enthusiasm, I imagined finally tidying up my workroom with her aid. I made a date with her for the next weekend and thanks to her help, I have finally started to clear up the piles of paper.

Lilly

I was excited to find out what fellow inhabitants I would run into in my home; I had never thought about such a thing before. One summer evening, I calmly sat down at the dining table, closed my eyes, and asked the beings in my house to show themselves. I invited them to congregate on the table; at first nothing happened, but I repeated my request with an expansive gesture of invitation and, lo and behold, two house elves were dancing on the tabletop. Things are a bit difficult with my roommates at the moment because two new people have moved in and are not respecting the rules, so I asked the house elves for support in the discussion that was to take place that evening. It worked. We were finally able to talk rationally with one another and work out a plan for getting the house tidy. Most importantly, all our reservations melted away.

Tina

When I was a little girl, my grandmother told me about Peter Pan and Tinkerbell the fairy. I really liked Tinkerbell and imagined her as a tiny, curious, headstrong, and cheerful little person. The boy who sat next to me in junior high used to torment me for a while, and one evening before falling asleep, I called out to Tinkerbell and asked her to sprinkle this boy with fairy dust so that he would stop annoying me. Somehow, it actually worked—my grammy always used to say, "Life is like in Neverland: you only have to believe in something completely in order to make it happen."

I have long since grown up, but Tinkerbell is still with me, and I have even introduced my young daughter to her. She has told me about a pink being with tiny wings and long blond hair who carries a magic wand. When this wand touches a wish, it can fly and come true. At the moment, she is wishing for a new best friend now that Sara has moved away. This too is dreaming with the essential power of Nature.

Katja

As I do every year, I sowed my tomato seeds in small planters in March and soon the first tiny seedlings appeared, ready for repotting. But then suddenly they stopped growing. I waited a few days and then got in touch with the tomato elf. Oh dear, I actually had to wake her up: she had failed to notice that spring had come. She quickly splashed some water on her eyes, shook herself, and got started on speeding up growth. I could actually see the tomato plants catching up.

The gods

Spirit beings also include the gods. Gods are beings with great power, self-confidence, and influence. Countless tales have been told of the gods; they have many faces, names, and abilities. They embody an ideal image that reminds us what powers and possibilities we harbor within us, and that we can use our divine potential to tread lightly and gracefully through life.

Gods and spirit beings give us the gift of their powers, ideas, wisdom, and desire to heal. They make new suggestions and give us the courage to use our natural force to view the opportunities life has to offer ever more clearly.

We encounter them whenever we go through life with our eyes open and direct our gaze toward the essential energy that resides in all things. A dog that is totally focused on chasing a rabbit is expressing exactly the same essential energy as a thunderstorm, or a bramble hedge's unbridled joy in growth.

Exercise: Another way of looking

Take a good look at an element and observe the divine within it, as though it were filled with radiant, resplendent energy. Take this divine energy into your heart. Looking at things in this way will bring the divine qualities within you closer to hand.

Exercise: Introduce the goddesses

Invite the goddess of each element into the center of your power circle. Notice the form in which she manifests herself, and be aware that you carry aspects of this goddess within you. Work through the list until you have become acquainted with all the goddesses; if you wish to use their names, please see page 17. Get a goddess involved in an issue that interests you.

Exercise: Get to know the gods of the elements

Hi'iaka is the goddess of wind. What message does she whisper to you when you dream of introducing a breath of fresh air into your life, or putting wind in the sails of a stagnating healing process? Call on the goddess that seems most suitable for the particular issue you are dealing with.

Real-life accounts

Lena

I'm a real cat fan, and Snappy and Dolores, my two cats, mean the world to me. I traveled around Morocco on my own this year, and the wild, half-starved cats that I saw there moved me to tears. There was always a cat running after me, sitting on my chair, or lying exhausted in the street. I could derive no joy from the beautiful landscape or in meeting people; the cats' suffering blotted out everything. I was totally aware that I couldn't save every last stray cat in Morocco, but I wanted to do more than just stroke or feed them every now and then.

As dawn rose, I sat down on the ground, entered my power circle, and called out to the goddess of the animals. I thought of my two little tigers at home and how much I love them, and this love for animals was intended as my way of establishing contact. It was my first encounter with the goddess of the animals, and I waited for her to appear with great excitement. A figure slowly appeared out of the mist; she was extremely beautiful and radiated indescribable love. I would describe her appearance as a kind of composite image of every animal. I explained my pain and asked for help. She suggested planting a seed of light in the hearts of all mankind. This seed would help to loosen deeply entrenched attitudes and to open people's eyes to the suffering of many animals. "Start in your own back-yard," she advised me.

I called to mind several people who like animals but don't get involved with them. I gave each of them a seed of light. She then said: "Give a seed to all those other people who are already on the right track." I am glad to have this point of contact now, and I shall return to it frequently.

Leander
I recently carried out a very simple ritual with the god of water. He revealed himself to me as a small, vibrant, gentle being living in a gushing spring. Having separated from my wife, I am feeling far from divine at the moment; my children don't want any contact with me and I don't know what to do. Although it was the right decision, I still feel pretty down; I simply needed divine power. I sat on the sofa, summoned the water god, and let his divine energy flow around me. I didn't want advice, I just wanted to be accepted, to be thought of as good, just as I am. It was so good for me, I can really recommend it in such situations.

Working with the symbolic power of Nature

Our lives are full of symbols: we make use of all kinds, from traffic signs, lights, and cairns to emoticons. Symbols have an effect on us; they are found in Nature in many different forms. Think of when you look at clouds in the sky and suddenly see a shape—an animal, a vehicle, a heart—which you interpret symbolically, making a link with it to your own life.

Symbols are their own kind of language; they inform and represent on many levels what can barely be expressed in words. Even the sight of a majestic mountain prompts a sense of size, power, invincibility, inner strength, and much more. When chosen wisely, a symbol from Nature can be a true source of power for us. Every natural symbol gives a sense of a new experience, new feelings, and a new form of power. Your body understands the language of symbols and perceives them as direct instruction. Imagine how you might feel after critical feedback from someone, say your line manager—small and helpless, with a knot in your stomach. When you go home, a dog barks loudly and attracts your attention. You watch it for a while and imagine being this agitated creature, defending your space and barring anything or anyone from approaching you. Your body does the rest and relieves the frustrations within you.

Exercise: Change your dreams

It is much more useful to change dreams rather than to interpret them. We think we have to find the meanings of dreams in order to feed our intellects, but I'd like to tell you about a very efficient method that has been tried and tested many times; it has produced good results with children who suffer nightmares and recurring bad dreams in particular. Think of a dream, and let the wind or another element change it. You'll be amazed at the story that is created as a result, and at the positive effects it will have.

Exercise: Facilitate access

We all have to deal with people that we are unable to get through to; we think of them as inaccessible. Imagine a thorn hedge in front of one such person, as a symbol of "access denied." Now take one of Nature's powers and make changes to this hedge; choose another type of hedge plant, or another shape, size, color, or position for the hedge, and see what happens in the future.

Exercise: Power image

An image of a power place, a powerful natural phenomenon, or a goddess has strong symbolic content; each such image radiates its own vibrations and energy. Place your hand on the image and observe what physical reactions follow; the energy of the picture will activate your energy, and your body can use this to dissolve blockages. Armed with this new knowledge, your collection of nature photographs will take on new meaning. I have put a power image under my bed so that I sleep soundly, completely relaxed, and full of the energies of Nature.

Exercise: Ask for a symbol

Think of something that you would like to make a reality and go outside into Nature. Ask for a symbol that will help you in your chosen endeavor. Go from element to element with open hands, and you'll be amazed at the symbol that awaits you as your gift at the end of this journey.

Exercise: Meet bold pioneers

Take a look around you: there are some bold pioneers living in your neighborhood. These are wild plants and creatures with elemental power. They bravely thrive on traffic islands, in nooks and crannies, in city dumps, and on asphalt streets. They make use of every opportunity to spread their seeds and face every challenge. These bold pioneers are what we call dandelions, stinging nettles, and plantains, or woodlice, ants, spiders, or slugs. They have no need of creature comforts and can handle anything: exhaust gases, damp, trash, or chemicals. There are bold pioneers wherever you go. When you see one, think of it as a symbol for courage, a sense of adventure, and perseverance. How can it help you?

Exercise: Open your eyes

Go outside into Nature and open your eyes. Look for an object that will put a spring in your step. Perhaps a leaf, a feather, a pine cone, or a blossom will attract your attention. When you get home, find a good place for your found object, perhaps in a pocket, depending on what type of object it is and its size.

Real-life accounts

Bridget

I like to visit my power circle in the mornings. I take a seat right in the middle and then run through my day in my mind: what is next in the diary, what challenges await, what am I looking forward to? Then I wait to see which element approaches me. This morning it was fire, so fire became my symbol for the day, and I ran through my agenda with the power of fire. During the day, I repeatedly took two or three conscious breaths of fire. Let's see what element will be by my side tomorrow.

Sabine

My daughter slept very badly when she started school. At the time, goosegrass was in bloom, and I had read somewhere that it was once used to promote good sleep. Together, my daughter and I picked some and wove a garland for her hair from it. We hung this garland symbolically over her bed. I told my daughter that the little white fairy from this plant would watch over her every night. She really liked this, and although she now sleeps deeply and well, the garland remains so the fairy will still visit.

Leo

I have had a recurring dream for years: I am in a different place each time, but am suddenly unable to walk. My legs are paralyzed and no matter what I do, I can't move them at all. The dream ends with this scene, and it was at exactly this point in the dream that I invited fire to take it further. To do this, I lit a candle. A small and agile fire elf began to hover around, driving me completely crazy. The longer I engaged with her, the greater I felt my ability to move. She gave me a sudden push and off I went, running freely and surefootedly, jumping and spinning around. It was an incredible feeling. Days later, I dug out my trainers, which had been down in the cellar for years, and decided I was going to do something for myself again, no matter how busy my diary looked.

Babs

We were heading off by car on vacation. My husband and the children were asleep and it was my turn to be behind the wheel for the next three hours. I had had a slight headache as we set off but it had become unbearable. I didn't want to take a break or have a sleep; being stuck in traffic with the children was not an appealing option. So I asked my head about its current dream, and instantly saw an image of a large airport display board, full of information that was constantly being updated. I didn't need to think too long about it; I wound down the window and let the wind blow over my head for as long as it took to be aware of a change. My husband woke up shortly afterward and asked if he should take over the driving. I shook my head. My headache had disappeared.

Reinforcing rituals with the energies of Nature

Rituals are part of our lives; they provide structure and security. When we get up in the morning, we follow a set course of actions. We make sure the light is out before we leave the house, celebrate the holiday season in a particular way, or read before falling asleep. Rituals are particularly appropriate when we want to emphasize something, implement change, or establish a new habit. A ritual carried out with the support of the elements simply has more power. Using the energies of Nature, a ritual becomes a sensual experience, and your subconscious values sensory pleasures highly. Our ancestors were aware of this and would celebrate rituals in harmony with the energies of Nature. Many of these have been preserved to this day, including Candlemas, the spring equinox, summer solstice, and Thanksgiving. We are reborn every day, and every ritual has the quality of a rebirth.

Combining everyday rituals with something you hope to achieve

We can link our daily rituals with a force of Nature and give them a meaning; this can turn simple actions such as boiling water or cleaning our teeth into significant and powerful activities. Run through the first half hour of your day in your mind and choose something that you do every day that has become a habit, such as turning on the coffee machine, cleaning your teeth, or airing your bed. Attach a meaning to this routine task. After getting up in the morning, I drink a cup of warm water; for me, this habit now means that I am immediately in the moment and can start the day wide awake. The power of the water reinforces my desire.

Ritual: Transformation

The elements shape the environment we live in and are masters of transformation. Thanks to photosynthesis, a single hundred-year-old tree produces around 28 pounds of oxygen every day, about as much as ten people might use up in 24 hours. Fire is voracious and consumes everything we feed it, creating fertile ashes. Animals exist in an eternal food chain of eating and being eaten. Every element is transformative. Choose an element and stimulate change by entrusting it with transforming an issue or situation that has lost momentum.

Ritual: Shapeshifting

A plant "dies" in winter and returns with new vigor in the spring. A water droplet soaks into the Earth, becomes water vapor, freezes, turns into snow, and then becomes a liquid drop of water once more. Snakes shed their skins, caterpillars turn into butterflies. The elements are expert at changing form. Use an element to change a habit or a role that you normally adopt: change the caterpillar into a butterfly, turn a very demanding and exhausting habit into a simple new everyday routine. Be inspired by the element you have chosen.

Ritual: Vision walking

Take a walk outdoors. Set a time limit and use the walk to gather inspiration and vision for one of your dreams. Don't worry, you don't have to note down everything you encounter, but you can be sure that certain things will attract your attention and capture your gaze. These will symbolically represent the issue you are interested in. While you are still out walking, or afterward, think about what you encountered and go home armed with the forces you have gathered.

Exercise:
Choose a plant to give an idea wings and let it fly

I love to do this exercise in the spring when everything is in bud. I choose an idea and combine its fulfillment with the growth of a plant that I see very often. In my mind, I have hung ideas on the apple tree, the forsythia hedge, or a dandelion. As I watch the plant grow, I feel joy at how my idea grows ever stronger every day. Why not try it, too.

Ritual: Activate your elemental force

We are an elemental force, although in our busy lives we may put this fact to the back of our minds, or even forget or lose sight of it completely. But we must uncover it, reflect on it, and bring it back to the fore; then we can be an elemental force once again, living out our elemental nature. Remember the story right at the beginning of this book: the brother of all humanity as a tuber. We can imagine a potato easily, a tuber that contains the elemental force of life within it; every seed, every shoot of a plant fulfils the same purpose. Plant one in the soil and see its primal power and presence as a symbol and a reminder of your own elemental power. A friend of mine does this every year when she plants potatoes.

Ritual: Family power circle

You can make a power circle for your family to complement your own power circle. You could even set one up for your company or a club that you are a member of. If your family should encounter difficulties, go through the power circle and check how each element is doing, reinforcing any that seem weaker in order to create greater harmony.

Ritual: Boost elemental power

The procedure for this ritual reminds me of taking an automobile through a car wash. It moves from section to section before emerging sparkling clean at the end. Instead of heading for the car wash, go to your power circle and run through the elements. Each element will do something to help: begin with your wind element and remain with it until you feel the urge to move on, and then keep going until you have gone through all seven elements. Now take a moment to sense your positive resonance.

Ritual: The comfort of elemental forces

Our lives are not always full of sunshine and roses; there are days when we are sad, discouraged, exhausted, disheartened, pessimistic, frightened, or angry, and when we find ourselves in such situations, the elemental forces can be of great comfort and help. Take your problems outside into Nature and allow each element to embrace and comfort you. Nature is a balm for our spiritual lives.

Lovely weather

Which of us is really in tune with the weather? It's often too warm, too wet, too dry, or too foggy; everything depends on the weather, especially if we've planned a vacation or an outdoor event. But dreaming that we are able to influence the climate is not such an absurd idea. Weather is created from an interplay of the elements, which is what makes weather forecasting so difficult: there are too many variable factors at play. We can exploit this very flexibility, however, and try to influence the weather. We cannot command the weather, that is undoubtedly beyond our abilities. No one has power over Nature. Each element has its own free will, just like us. All we can do is suggest to Nature that it does something a little more or less powerfully. You can ask snow clouds to move away slightly more quickly, or the wind to use all its might to bring the rain clouds for which you've been waiting for so long. You might turn to the sun when you would like some blue sky over the path you intend to walk. The weather will always cooperate with our suggestions wherever it can; we are all a part of Nature and influence one another, whether we know it or not. When we work with the weather, we are using this influence entirely consciously.

Ritual: Make friends with the weather

Get in tune with the weather and express your appreciation. Praise what you feel is good about it. Talk to the weather; say hello. For example, you might say: "Hello sun, thank you for your warmth, it's doing me good."

Now think about the different ways in which the weather can help you. Visualize the blue sky above you and show how the weather can help ensure that the guests at your barbecue have a good time. Experience the images you create with every sense. Say thank you for the weather's cooperation and you can expect the best.

Real-life accounts

Lena

I carried out the "comfort of elemental forces" ritual with my young son. We were spending a few days at the coast and he was missing his dad. I wanted to do something nice for him so I told him he should imagine his sorrow becoming lighter and lighter. We were walking on the shore and he stood in the wind. His fire power was a Star Wars light saber and he jumped in a puddle wearing rubber boots. He plucked some grass from the dunes as a plant, and he played with the sand. His animal was of course the brontosaurus buried deep below us, and the whole thing was rounded off with a Superman action figure. An odd combination, but it did the trick.

Sam

I am experiencing some bullying right now, so I took the worried part of me through my power circle in order to regain a sense of security. I happened to be at an open-air swimming pool; first the wind blew around me, then I talked for a while with a sunbeam, I swam in the pool, and then walked across the grass with mindfulness, I sat down on the ground, and watched a bee trying to taste my neighbor's ice cream. I finally asked God to make my remaining insecurity vanish.

Mandy

I always thought it was impossible to change the weather, but I wanted to try for my son's wedding. After a long year of illness, I wished him a beautiful spring wedding in the sunshine. That morning, I sat down in peace and thanked the sun for its warmth and for making the plants grow. Then I asked for its help and invited it to shine over our town for the whole day. I saw us stepping out of the church into the sunshine and at the photoshoot in the park, and saw how the children could play out-doors. I concentrated hard on the joy that the presence of the sun would bring. I was so proud of myself; despite an uncertain forecast, it didn't start raining until the evening.

Frances

I was making use of my evening stroll along the creek for a vision walk; I was dawdling, letting my thoughts wander, and thinking how I have been sidelined in our women's group since I stopped blindly agreeing to everything, I have felt some women distancing themselves from me. I like being involved with the group, and would like people to accept me as I am. Three brown slugs caught my attention, and I got down on my knees and inspected them more closely. Unimpressed with my presence, they carried on their journey. People don't like them, and yet they stay just as they are, going about their business slowly and steadily, without complaint. If there's a long dry spell, they find a shady spot. They put out their feelers to find the best route, and can sniff out tasty treats.

Yes, I could be like this slug, slowly showing my new side and stretching out my feelers to those who accept me and don't expect me to be "everybody's darling." And if it all gets a bit much for me, I can retreat into the shade. The slugs made me hopeful that slowly but surely my situation could change.

Tanya

I like to drink tea during the day, which has prompted me to develop my own tea ceremony. I have integrated all the elements into it. Water is my basic ingredient, combined with the energy of plants from the tea leaves. The warmth of the tea represents fire energy; the cup symbolizes the element of rocks; stirring activates the power of the wind; and the honey in the tea adds animal energy. Combined with all this is the creative energy of Nature.

Enjoy! All seven elements in one cup of power tea. I sense a little more of my elemental power with every sip, and want to reinforce this with the ritual.

I told a friend about the ritual and she has adopted the idea in her own way: blow-drying her hair every day brings her the power of the air with a view to ending her single days and putting fresh wind in her sails.

MALAMA PONO:
LOOK AFTER YOURSELF!

This is how the Hawaiian people say goodbye and I shall do the same. Living every minute with the energies of Nature is amazing: allow them to play an active and immediate part in everything you do as you become more alive and more powerful. What at first seemed an unattainable dream will become reality in the most wonderful way. You can reinvent your life with these powerful partners at your side. Combine your strength with the power and energy of water spirits, animal beings, stone goblins, fire dragons, wind fairies, plant elves, and gods. It will give new momentum to your daily life and turn you into a "rock in the surf"; you will experience more energy and joy in your life as you enjoy your newfound drive and love of life in this beautiful world. Enjoy this firework display of powers and potential every single day and whenever you feel like it, ask yourself: "What new projects and undiscovered opportunities are out there waiting for me?"

Malama Pono! Listen to the voices of the energies of Nature, who will be whispering these wise and sensible words of wisdom so that everything goes well for you.

Wind message

Change your point of view,
Treat yourself to a fresh breeze,
Make sure you have a following wind,
Be daring!

Fire voice

Be a flame for your ideas,
Burn brightly for life,
Burn with passion,
Burn forever!

Water impulses

Don't get bent out of shape,
Always keep moving,
Change what gets in your way,
Enjoy your journey!

Plant thoughts

Grow into the light,
Put down roots in good soil,
Enjoy your beauty,
Heal yourself!

A stone speaks
Live in balance,
Watch and learn,
Store sunlight,
Never stop looking after your wellbeing!

Advice from the animal kingdom
Take pleasure in life,
Make decisions quickly,
Speed up and pause for a second,
Follow your intuition!

A message from the creatures of nature
Be airy and light in your thinking,
Carefree and curious in your actions,
Intense and wise in your feelings,
And loud and insatiable when you laugh;
Fill your life with enjoyment and expectation!

Disclaimer

The information in this book is given in good faith and is not intended to diagnose any physical or mental condition or serve as a substitute for informed medical advice or care. Please contact your health professional for medical advice and treatment. Neither author nor publisher can be held liable by any person for any loss or damage whatsoever that may arise from the use of this book or any of the information therein.

About the author

Susanne Weikl is a registered naturopath (psychotherapy) and Alaka'i (Huna teacher), having trained with Aloha International, Hawaii. After spending many years in the HR department of a bank, she followed her heart and devoted herself to her healing  work. Her love of travel has brought her into contact with healers all over the world; in her own practice in Neu-Ulm, she helps people in individual sessions, seminars, and training courses to become a Huna Practitioner®, and she also organizes seminar trips to Hawaii and South Africa. Nature is her greatest source of inspiration and the elemental forces of Nature are her best friends. The teachings of Huna, with its emphasis on harmony, are an essential part of her life. She has studied Hawaii with Serge Kahili King, who found fame with his book *Urban Shaman* and is an expert on Huna. Her book *Harmony in Three Minutes* is one of the best introductions to Huna philosophy. Susanne Weikl looks on life as a great adventure and helps people to live life dynamically, instead of merely existing.

The heart, often perceived as our most vulnerable and fragile place, is in fact the source of our greatest potential. This book will unveil the seven secret powers of the heart and help you to discover how you can awaken them. This will lead you to a deep sense of peace, balance, and fulfilment and enable you to approach life from a place of trust and love.

Shai Tubali
Unlocking the Seven Secret Powers of the Heart
A practical guide to living in trust and love
Paperback, full color throughout, 128 pages
ISBN 978-1-62055-812-6

Discover everything you need to know about the luminous infinity symbol. Use the many simple exercises contained in this book for decision-making, improving your relationships, reconnecting the analytical and the emotional sides of your brain, and much more. The lemniscate can be used in a wide variety of ways.

Barbara Heider-Rauter
The Power of the Infinity Symbol
Working with the lemniscate for ultimate harmony and balance
Paperback, full color throughout, 128 pages
ISBN 978-1-84409-752-4

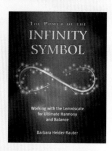

Both Ho'oponopono, the Hawaiian forgiveness ritual, and family constellation therapy help to heal our relationships with the world around us and bring healing to our inner world. This hands-on book brings together what belongs together, providing beginners with an introduction and easy access to the subject and the more experienced with fresh insights.

Ulrich Emil Duprée
Ho'oponopono
A traditional Hawaiian healing method
for relationships, forgiveness, and love
Paperback, full color throughout, 160 pages
ISBN 978-1-84409-717-3

This powerful book with its beautiful illustrations allows you to enter the mystical world of dragons. Once you are ready, it will help you get to know your own dragon, your close personal companion, and to share its invincibility, wisdom, and magic.

Christine Arana Fader
The Little Book of Dragons
Finding your spirit guide
Paperback, full color throughout, 120 pages
ISBN 978-1-84409-670-1

Healing Crystals is a comprehensive and up-to-date directory of 555 healing gemstones, presented in a practical and handy pocket guide format. In the revised edition of his bestseller, Michael Gienger, famous for his pioneering work in the field of crystal healing, describes the characteristics and healing powers of each crystal in a clear, concise, and precise style, accompanied by four-color photographs.

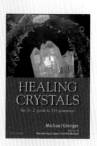

Michael Gienger
Healing Crystals
the A–Z guide to 555 gemstones, 2nd edition
Paperback, full color throughout, 128 pages
ISBN 978-1-84409-647-3

This pocket pharmacy of healing stones embraces many applications. Although describing only twelve stones, the breadth of its scope resembles a home pharmacy. From allergies to toothache, you will find the right stone for every application. This handy little book offers you the essence of our modern knowledge of healing stones.

Michael Gienger
Twelve Essential Healing Crystals
Your first aid manual for preventing and treating common ailments from allergies to toothache
Paperback, full color throughout, 64 pages
ISBN 978-1-84409-642-8

Powerful yet concise, this revolutionary guide summarizes the
Hawaiian ritual of forgiveness and offers methods for immediately
creating positive effects in everyday life. Ho'oponopono consists of four
consequent magic sentences: "I am sorry. Please forgive me. I love you.
Thank you." By addressing issues using these simple sentences we get
to own our feelings, and accept unconditional love, so that unhealthy
situations transform into favorable experiences.

Ulrich Emil Duprée
Ho'oponopono
The Hawaiian forgiveness ritual as
the key to your life's fulfilment
Paperback, full color throughout, 96 pages
ISBN 978-1-84409-597-1

Ho'oponopono
and Family
Constellations
*A traditional Hawaiian healing method
for relationships, forgiveness and love*
Ulrich E. Duprée

Gem water can be a valuable aid to health, providing effective remedies
and acting quickly on a physical level. Water is known to carry mineral
information, so by placing crystals in water it becomes charged with
the crystals' energy. Drinking gem water as a therapeutic treatment is
similar and complementary to wearing crystals, although the effects are
not necessarily the same.

Gem Water should be prepared and used with care; this book explains
everything you need to know to get started.

Michael Gienger, Joachim Goebel
Gem Water
How to prepare and use more than
130 crystal waters for therapeutic treatments
Paperback, full color throughout, 96 pages
ISBN 978-1-84409-131-7

Gem
Water
How to prepare and use
more than 130 crystal waters
for therapeutic treatments
Michael Gienger
Joachim Goebel

For further information and to request a book catalog contact:

Inner Traditions, One Park Street, Rochester, Vermont 05767

Earthdancer Books is an Inner Traditions imprint.
Phone: +1-800-246-8648, customerservice@innertraditions.com
www.earthdancerbooks.com • www.innertraditions.com